By Cory Kruse

A Dream of Darkness
(The Norick Saga, Book 1)

Grace in the Dirt:
Poems, Songs, and Other
Reflections on Life

GRACE
IN THE DIRT

*Poems, Songs, and
Other Reflections on Life*

GRACE
IN THE DIRT

by
Cory Kruse

FIRE'S EDGE
PUBLISHING

Copyright © 2021 by Cory Kruse

All rights reserved. No portion of this book may be reproduced, stored in a retrieval system, or transmitted in any form or by any means—electronic, mechanical, photocopy, recording, or any other—except for brief quotations in printed reviews, without the prior written permission of the publisher. Thank you for your support of the author's rights.

Fire's Edge Publishing
310 N. Derby Lane PO Box 800
North Sioux City, SD 57049

First Edition: December 2021

ISBN 978-1-7330694-4-1 (paperback)
ISBN 978-1-7330694-5-8 (e-book)
Library of Congress Control Number: 2021908031

Cover Art, Typesetting, and Interior Book Design by Anamaria Stefan
Proofreading by Parisa Zolfaghari

To learn more, visit AuthorCoryKruse.com

Printed in the United States of America

For every girl who broke my heart,

And for the One who never will.

I am unjust, but I can strive for justice.
My life's unkind, but I can vote for kindness.
I, the unloving, say life should be lovely.
I, that am blind, cry out against my blindness.

— Vachel Lindsay, excerpt from
"Why I Voted the Socialist Ticket"

Contents

xv
Preface

or

The Humility, and Vanity, of
Diary Sharing

1
Love

or

The Song of a
Cultivated Heart

121
Loss

or

The Lament of a
Ravaged Field

265
Despair

or

The Ache of a
Fallow Soul

489
Hope

or
The Promise of a
Buried Seed

691
Acknowledgments

or
The Sowers and the One
Who Reaped

711
About the Author

or
The Farmer
and His Harvest

GRACE
IN THE DIRT

PREFACE

Or

The Humility, and Vanity,
of Diary Sharing

Confession and Concealment
Are twin siblings at war.

Bitter rivals,
They vie endlessly
For dominion within us.

One calls for release,
For trust,
The freedom found in unburdening.

While the latter urges silence,
Safety,
The comfort of a carefully curated life.

Thus,
For every story told,
For every weakness shared,
Another goes neglected:
Left tucked away
And buried in darkness.

I've never really been one for keeping a diary.

And it's not that I don't understand the impulse—after all, what could be more important than the preservation of your memories, your experiences, all those little moments of minutia and mundanity interspersed with the more elevated occasions of wonder and tragedy? A diary attempts to capture at least a small part of that tapestry: the infinity of moments, both large and small, that make up a life. My own reticence toward the activity stems, as best as I can surmise, from an ongoing scuffle I hold with perfectionism. Penning journal entries day after day simply feels like another obligation, yet one more task in which I'll need to strive for flawlessness and precision. Which kind of defeats the purpose then, doesn't it? How truthful can a diary be when its author is hyperaware of his inner critic? Won't such incessant overthinking inherently mar the exercise, as that author endeavors—subconsciously or otherwise—to paint himself and his experiences in a certain light?

Likewise, I'm left to wonder: Can't the very existence of a diary, in one manner or another, actually end up influencing how a person lives their life? Won't certain thoughts and behaviors inevitably result, prompted by the knowledge you'll be writing about them later on?

Talk about overthinking, right? Trust me, I know.

Gestures broadly

Welcome to my mind.

Reservations aside, the fact remains: I'm a writer, and, as such, I naturally express myself *through writing*. As obvious as that statement may sound, it's imperative for understanding how this book came about. While maintaining a formal diary doesn't much interest me (i.e., the prospect continues to overwhelm me), I still require some sort of outlet for my thoughts and feelings. The obvious solution would be to use my fictional work as such a release, and it certainly does afford an avenue for that—to an extent. I've found writing of that sort seems to work on a more primal, subconscious level. And not to mention it's much more time-intensive, which means it doesn't exactly lend itself to day-to-day concerns or ruminations. So, where does that leave me? How do I process those everyday emotions and experiences? How do I express myself?

Enter: my cellphone's Notes app.

I realize how "millennial" of me that sounds, but it's the truth, and I figure I can't be alone. There's just something about the format that inherently invites openness and honesty—and, most importantly, invites *use*. The pressure's off; the composition feels easier. A few quick keystrokes upon your touchscreen's digital keyboard, and suddenly you have a finished diary entry. You can work through your feelings in real time, in an almost stream-of-consciousness-like manner, without fretting over the strictures of grammar or syntax or even the completeness of a thought. You can just *write*—and for me, that is freedom.

Thus, for years, I've been pouring my heart out into that little virtual notepad, feverishly typing away any time my imagination is sparked or I wish to make sense of an event. Most of the entries are bite-size snippets: glimpses into how I was feeling at any given moment. Others contain mini stories or personal vignettes. And intermingled with all of these are longer reflections that explore deeper issues and truths; a bit of soul-searching, if you will.

Over the years, those notes have covered a wide range of human experiences: from the riotous, rosy-eyed euphoria of first love to the smothering, light-sucking chasms of failure, loneliness, and loss. I've waxed poetic on all the confusion and angst surrounding burgeoning adolescence. I've reflected on that aimless, detached feeling one gets after entering into adulthood and discovering that the world isn't as receptive to your dreams as you'd once hoped; that life is, at its core, much simpler than you'd imagined—and, at the same time, much more complicated: both a wellspring of freedom and a cage of responsibility.

So, too, have I navigated seasons of doubt and existential despair. I've lodged angry, self-righteous complaints at God; I've worshipped and supplicated and proclaimed my thanks. I've lamented the gray-skyed doldrums of depression, and the guilt I feel, however erroneously, over wasting my life because of it. I've mourned friends taken far too soon; I've quailed over the apparent trajectory of this broken, wayward world. I've confessed every character flaw and personal weakness: all those moments of temptation and backsliding and misplaced anxiety; all those instances of self-loathing, and the suffocating feeling of inadequacy that perpetually clouds my days.

Through it all, nevertheless, I have hoped. I have dreamed. I have memorialized crushes and triumphs and all manner of beautiful things. I have *paid attention*, as best as I am able: a witness to the quiet grandeur found within a single human life.

And now ...

Now, I'm sharing it all.

Okay, maybe not *all* of it.

For one thing, that would necessitate a book large enough to scare away even the most voracious of readers. And who in their right mind would even *want* to read an unfiltered account of another person's life? If I'm sure of anything, it's that slogging through an endless sluice of word vomit wouldn't be much fun for anyone. Nor is it likely to endear that author to too many of his fellow human beings. Trust me, some things are just better left unshared.

Which leads us to the crux of the matter: Why, then, am I publishing any of this? What value will you, as the reader, gain from continuing on through these pages? In other words, why should you care?

Good question.

You see, I recognize diary sharing is, at its core, an exercise both in humility *and* in vanity. On one hand, it takes courage to lay yourself bare, to peel back the layers of your public façade and reveal the landscape of your inner life: all those faults and fears, loves and longings; all those mistakes and soul-crushing failures; all those moments of profound feeling, and the central, deep-seated tenets that make you who you are. And there's no telling what the response toward such candor will be. I'm convinced one of the primal fears of all human beings is the fear of rejection. To be fully *seen* ... then deemed unworthy. We all yearn to be accepted, to be loved, and so we tuck parts of ourselves away, an instinctual defense mechanism, letting only our best qualities sift to the surface. We hide in broad daylight, terrified at the thought of exposing our authentic selves. Preservation through suppression. Safety through silence. Thus, the idea of being open, of being vulnerable, naturally grates at every fiber of our being—nails on a chalkboard, a tornado siren's urgent wailing—and requires a willingness to abandon your pride, to set aside your ego, and open yourself up to the world's judgment and scrutiny.

No easy feat. So, it takes courage—and perhaps a certain degree of recklessness.

On the other hand, I appreciate the narcissism inherent within such an enterprise. Divulging the contents of your diary—no matter what form that might take—is, in itself, an act of presumption, one that assumes a good number of things, not the least of which is that you, perhaps more than anyone, somehow merit society's consideration (or, if not its consideration, then at the very least its attention). As though you're some sort of celebrity, a person of significance, someone whose every thought and deed are of note. It presumes you *have something to say*, and that other people will care to hear it.

That your experiences, and the insights you've gleaned from them, will somehow complement their own, lending value in an increasingly crowded (and noisy) entertainment world.

All of which again begs the question: Why share this book? Why risk needless scrutiny, and potential misunderstandings, and the ever-present likelihood of coming off as some self-absorbed narcissist—all for the sake of releasing what, in the end, amounts to little more than a compilation of a digital diary?

The answer is simple: because I believe stories matter, regardless of to whom they might belong, and that there is value in their telling, both for the receiver *and* for the teller. While I make no illusions about being some kind of cultural icon or distinguished personality—quite the opposite, in fact—I've felt called to share my story nonetheless, believing, as ever, that there's power in vulnerability. Writing is a cathartic activity, but I've found sharing can be a *transformative* one. Through it, I can find grace and peace and healing. I can find acceptance, and support, and the brimming, transcendent joy of human connection. I can show others that—as the old platitude goes—"It's okay not to be okay," and that they, too, can be vulnerable.

I can show them, above all, that they're not alone.

I'm just a simple man—there's no getting around that—but maybe my very ordinariness is, in itself, an asset. Something to be leveraged, not shied away from. Maybe the everyday realities of my life can, in some small, ineffable way, speak to the experiences of other "ordinary" people. Maybe those realities can even help them. I would never profess to comprehend all of the things people go through, but I do believe some experiences are universal, if not in form then in function, and thus the stories of others can serve as common ground from which we can all find, and create, meaning. From those stories, we can ponder the larger truths, struggles, and general *messiness* of life. We can find strength, and hope. We can learn and practice empathy. And, through it all, we can grow in connection, no matter how removed that link may initially seem.

Perhaps all of that reads a bit like delusions of grandeur. Maybe so. But if there's one thing I've learned in this life, it's that you should never underestimate the power of storytelling, nor take for granted just how far one simple tale might go. Call me clichéd; call me a fool; call me a hopeless romantic; call me *whatever*—either way, I still believe stories can change the world.

And so here I am, telling mine.

If there's a second thing I've learned in this life, it's that life is full of contradictions.

Our joyride on this big, spinning blue ball is one fraught with inconsistencies, not the least of which is *us*. For human beings are fickle creatures, are we not? We're constantly changing, evolving, ping-ponging back and forth between any number of interests, personalities, and desires. Not to mention we're *complex*. Our minds are strange and wonderful and all too labyrinthine—often, *we* don't even know what we want nor how to get it. There are layers upon layers within us, an iceberg of competing identities clambering for the surface, constantly flipping over, one on top of the other, in an endless roil. Some of those identities eventually calve off ... and are lost forever. Others melt down and coalesce with their counterparts, forming a new sculpture altogether. We're continually recreating ourselves, then, while, at the same time, some parts of us never really change. Consequently, our sense of *self* exists somewhere on a sliding scale, a continuum, and that fact leads to all sorts of intriguing oddities.

We enjoy something, only to despise it a short time later. We fall madly in love ... only to wind up loathing the other person. We idolize careers, passions, celebrities ... only to feel that admiration inevitably sour. We hate liars, yet we spin innumerable white lies. We long for peace, yet we start wars. We bemoan injustice, yet we rarely work for change. We relish kindness, yet we so often neglect to lend it out. We demand forgiveness, yet we confine others to the stocks. We applaud passion, yet we wallow in apathy. We fear being alone, yet, from others, we regularly close ourselves off.

We ache for love while, at the same time, doubting we'll ever deserve it.

Like I said, life is full of contradictions. *People* are full of contradictions. And that's okay—we're complex, wonderful, *strange* creatures. We're profound and we're silly and we're the universe's grandest collection of utter fools. The sooner we embrace those facts—the sooner we accept the reality of our own imperfection, and all the inconsistencies that come along with it—the sooner we'll come to know ourselves fully, and we'll start to truly *live*.

Even from a more macro perspective, life is replete with head-spinning contradictions. The rising sun chases away the darkness. The winter snows silence summer's lush greenery. Effervescent rainbows follow after a destructive storm. Old age begins creeping the moment we're born.

The wicked prosper; the righteous toil. Faith is found in unholy places. Rip-roaring good days of joy and splendor are apportioned between yet longer spells of tedium, heartbreak, and tragedy. Peace breeds indolence. Wealth begets poverty. Freedom curdles into greed.

Water can drown, stagnate, or seed.

Such is the tension at the heart of this book: confession vs. concealment. Creation versus destruction. Love vs. hate. Faith versus fear. Moreover, I've come to learn life rarely works in binaries or neatly hewn dichotomies. Things are seldom, if ever, rendered strictly in black and white. So, while I'm not sure if there are fifty, a dozen, or even a hundred different shades, I do believe life is most often experienced in gray. This book dwells in that space of ambiguity, in the ambivalence and the impermanence, and finds me grappling with the effects of that muddle.

Therefore, it's a book about searching for beauty even in the darkest of places, in those bleakest of moments, right there in the midst of catastrophe. It's about doubt and wandering. It's about clinging to hope when there seems to be none, about being so lost in the mud and the grime that you barely possess the strength to clear away your eyes. It's about seeking forgiveness, even when you can't forgive yourself. It's about posing life's fundamental questions, even the uncomfortable ones, interrogating the universe and God and the deepest reaches of our inner selves, because to simply choose ignorance, to fester in apathy, would be the even greater affront.

It's about hunting for meaning, even in all the wrong places. It's about celebrating love, even the kind that doesn't last. It's about discovering grace, even in the wake of our greatest failures.

In other words, it is a snapshot of a typical human life, with all the inconsistencies and untidiness that goes along with it. As imperfect as it may be, this is my story—a small piece of it, anyway—and, I trust, it may be some of yours too.

A quick word on the book's format.

As a novelist by trade, I couldn't resist structuring the entries in such a way that they would adopt the semblance of a narrative, building one off the other to a natural—and hopefully satisfying—conclusion. As we all know, however, life is much messier than that, rarely affording us clear endings, permanent victories, or tidy, bow-capped moments of closure. Even so, I wanted these pages to contain a sense of momentum, of sequence, one that would progress the book's through-line in a type of literary journey. That isn't to say these entries are fictional; they're not. Rather, they're simply arranged in the order that made the most narrative sense, regardless of when they were first composed.

Likewise, some of the issues presented are things I've since overcome; the same is true for certain crushes and professions of love. Again, this book is meant to be a snapshot, an honest portrayal of how I was feeling at certain moments in my life as well as what mattered most during those junctures. So, while some of these reflections are no longer directly applicable, that doesn't diminish their significance either, as they were still pertinent steps along my life's journey, vital pieces that forged me into who I am today. Like all people, I've changed over the years; but, in so many ways, I've also stayed the same. This book reflects that metamorphosis, that pendulum swing of alternating identities, beliefs, desires, and character growth.

Simply put: While these words are now carved in stone—er, ink—the life responsible for them remains fluid.

Additionally, I want to briefly address the topic of faith, which recurs with some degree of frequency across these pages. While I consider myself a Christian, this is by no means intended to be a theological text. It's merely the musings of an everyday believer (read: a chronic, recurrent sinner) who's the furthest thing from wise, prophetic, or perfect. Each of these reflections was initially penned for my own benefit; they include my personal prayers, my 3:00 a.m. doubts, my revelatory truths, and my ever-shifting paradigms. They're the fruit of countless hours of soul-searching and spiritual wrestling; you can think of them as my own makeshift Psalms. Whether or not you subscribe to the same belief system as I do, I trust you'll be able to derive some measure of value from these reflections; if not, feel free to page right on past 'em.

The majority of the entries herein are poetic or lyrical in nature. A few are little more than bumper stickers or pithy sayings, truths I wished to cement for myself and am now passing along to you. I'm not much of a poet—at least not in the traditional sense—so I've done my best to keep each entry accessible. I also committed myself to being as authentic as possible. Just remember, however: My inner critic didn't just up and vanish. He's still in there somewhere, niggling away, overthinking with every breath. Be aware, then, that some degree of curation *has* occurred.

You wouldn't want to know everything anyway, remember?

To close then, this is a book—a diary—about finding light in the darkness. About discovering meaning in the madness; peace in the anguish; grace in the failures; beauty in the despair. It's about faith, hope, and love—and, as that one legendary tome once famously remarked, "... the greatest of these is love."

As always, I'm grateful for all of you, and I hope you enjoy the journey—this perilous voyage into vulnerability and connection and discovery. Travel alongside me, and I promise it will be worth the ride.

Let's go find grace in the dirt, together.

GRACE IN
THE DIRT

I'm searching for grace in the dirt,
Dirtying my hands, knowing it'll hurt.

I'm longing for love of a precious kind,
Scouring the world for what may never be mine.

I'm yearning for a peace beyond my grasp,
Begging for healing, praying it'll last.

Yeah, I'm searching for grace in the dirt,
'Cause I've learned there's treasure to be found buried in earth.
And because maybe dirty nails are better than nothing at all.
At least there's motion to every stagger and fall.

Once there was a time when I'd look toward the sky,
But from those lonesome stars, all I ever got was silence
In reply.

Yeah, I'm still searching for grace in the dirt—
Wondering, above all, what I might be worth.

LOVE

Or

The Song of a Cultivated Heart

*A heart, well-tended,
Is fertile ground.*

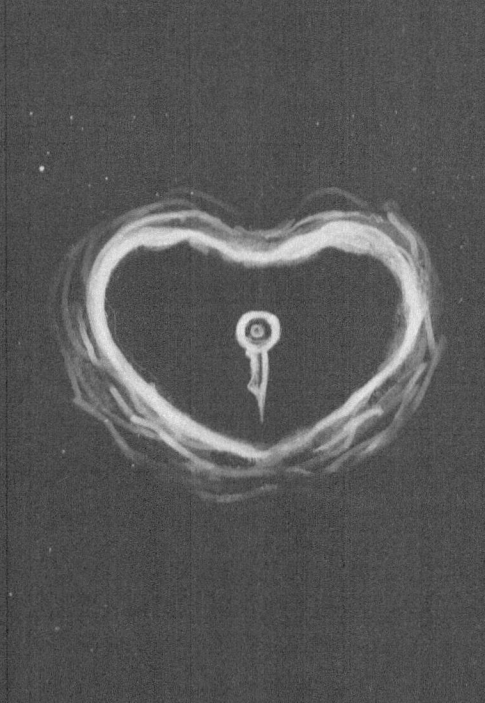

The First and the Last

Love: life's greatest mystery,
And its simplest directive.

Love: the answer to it all.

The Big Bang

It was Love who spun the universe into motion;
It's love that'll spark this body into life.

It was Love who gifted the world its color;
It's love that'll scrub the scales from these eyes.

It was Love who taught the day its wonder;
It's love that'll draw meaning from night.

It is Love who will save us all;
It's love that'll win this fight.

DNA

Disparate though our lives may be,
One truth remains—
In each of us is sown a common desire,
Some central tenet of our programming:

We yearn, each of us,
To love and to be loved.
And thus: to know, and to be known.

We ache for something real,
Something true,
A place these broken hearts
Can call home.

Storm Chaser

I'm waiting on the rain
I'm begging for a storm
I wanna feel the thunder
And static on my arms

Give me wind-tossed hair
And rain-soaked flesh
Let the surge pull me under:
Heave, enfold, press

Yes, let the storm take me
Let the waves steal my breath
Let me lose myself in the roil
And find freedom in the depths

Nature vs. Nurture

Do I settle for what isn't true?
Or do I hold out hope that, one day,
True love will come breaking through?

Creed

In my opinion, the person with whom you end up should be someone who brings out the very best in you. Somebody with whom you can be completely yourself; who makes every hour feel like a minute and every minute like an hour.

That person should, without a doubt, be your best friend.

"Already Seen"

Will it feel like déjà vu
When I first lock eyes with you?

Will your voice sound familiar?
Will it hit like an old childhood rhyme?
Will our hearts be drawn together?
Will your soul at once recognize mine?

Will I love you from the beginning,
With the weight of years gone by?
Will I merely be *continuing* our story,
The moment I stammer out, "Hi"?

Either / Or

Maybe I'll find the one
Maybe she'll find me
Maybe "The One"
Is just something we were raised to believe

Maybe our paths will cross at a bar
Maybe I'll sit by her at church
Maybe it'll start as friendship
Or as some great, stomach-tossing lurch

Maybe it'll blossom slow like spring flowers
Or dart quick like June butterflies
Maybe it'll sneak upon me gradually
Or come the moment I gaze into her eyes

Maybe our love will be a mundane affair
A foundation built solid on practicality and routine
Maybe our tale will be one for the ages
The greatest love story this world has ever seen

Maybe the one, whoever she is,
Will learn all my secrets and my scars
Maybe she'll still accept me
Even as she maps the topography of my heart

Maybe I'll find her, or maybe I won't
Either she's out there, or I'll wind up alone
Either way, I'll go on searching
Right up until the Good Lord

Calls me home

Who Would've Thought?

Our hearts land
In unexpected places

Comets

We were spinning in different orbits
You and I

But just a glimpse as you passed
Was enough to ignite the sky

Push / Pull

I felt it before I understood it.
Recognized it, as sure as the tides
Know the pull of the moon:

I was made for you.

Just Comes Natural

You get my heart a-thumpin'
My tongue, tangled and glued

You've earned every bit of my love, girl
Without even trying to

All Day Long

Your hair is a waving sunflower
Or maybe a patch of straw
It drinks up the brightest sunshine
And gifts light back to us all

Your nose is a loaded coil
Crinkles with disgust, and with laughter
The image of it still fills my mind
All these countless days after

Your voice is the sweetest melody
And your heart, the purest song
Even a word or two is enough
Enough to get me dancin'
All day long

In Case You Didn't Know

Do you know how great you are,
How beautiful your eyes?
Do you know you live inside my head
And light up my dreams at night?

Do you know your laughter soothes like medicine;
Your kindness, like the sweetest nectar?
Do you know you could change the world
With just one snap of your lovely fingers?

Do you know you arouse wonder
And devotion of the religious sort?
Do you know I love you completely,
My first and last resort?

Light Bringer

You fill my soul
With light

Love Is Proximity

I had no prior ambitions; my heart, no grand design.
When I strolled into the room that day,
It wasn't love I'd meant to find.

But there you were in all your glory, as perfect as can be:
Eyes as sharp as glass;
Voice as smooth as honey.

I soaked up every moment, lost track of all my time.
Found infinity in our encounters,
And magic in your shine.

I'm not sure what drew us together, nor what fused these lonely hearts,
But I know it was heaven when you were around
And a wasteland when we were apart.

Yeah, it's heaven when you're around,
But a wasteland when we're apart.

Comfort Zones

You were waiting for me;
I was waiting on you.

But neither of us could bring ourselves
To make that first move.

Games

You have me faking run-ins
When I know just where you'll be
You have me posting pictures, chasing likes,
Just praying that you'll see

You have me changing my outfit
At least half a dozen times
Have me at the mirror
Testing out all my corny lines

We play these games
We dance that dance
We flirt with fire
With every secret glance

We keep on circling
Like it's the chase we're addicted to
Neither of us willing to let go
As though we're both afraid to lose

We play these games
And maybe that's all right
For even if it's only games
At least I'm in your life

Circumstantial Evidence

Secret glances
And lovers' smiles ...

That lead to nothing at all.

Stupid grins
And poker faces ...

Excuses to cross paths in the hall.

Online flirting
And subtle clues ...

A bluff neither of us will ever call.

Stolen days
And unspoken goodbyes ...

Love lost in time's eternal crawl.

Soured memories
And countless *what-ifs* ...

Two strangers who could've had it all.

Girl,
We could've had it all.

Convergence

We're twin suns
Orbiting each other:

Your light is my light
My warmth, yours

But the same gravity that holds us together
Is the very same thing
That keeps us apart

K.C.

I loved you from afar
That's probably something you never knew
I'll love you from afar
Even if that's all I ever get to do

I loved you from afar
Cheering you every step of the way
I'll love you from afar
Right up to my dying day

Better to Have Loved and Been Friend-Zoned Than Never to Have Loved at All

Is love left unrequited
Still worth it in the end?
Was it all just a waste,
If I'm only ever your friend?

I hear my heart answer,
Its words soft and true:
"Yes, it was worth it,
If only for what it did to you."

The Journey, Not the Destination

Love, on its own,
Is reward enough.

I Didn't Plan on You

There it is,
That old familiar spark:
Magic found in a stranger's eyes.

There it is,
The one thing that could convince me
To give love another try.

There it is; there it is.

Conversational Soulmates

We met at a bar, at least the first time.
You were there with some friends; I was there with mine.

Our groups came together; had a mutual friend or two.
Soon you were standing before me, and I swear I couldn't get enough of you.

We shared pitchers and straw-bound races.
We laughed at each other's struggle, our collective pinched faces.

We talked Eric Church and double albums and the trilogy found in those songs.
We traded drinking stories and favorites memories
And debated *Star Wars* movies for far too long.

We talked for what felt like hours in that smoky, neon-soaked room.
We leaned our heads together, bobbing along to every '90s country tune.

We talked for what felt like hours ... but soon the night came to an end.
You told me, "I think I might love you." I just laughed
And begged to see you again.

Friday Morning Chats

Is it crazy to say I might love you?
Am I out of my mind if I do?

Is it right that the best part of my day
Is standing by that vending machine, just talking to you?

I love learning about your favorite movies.
I love swapping our discovered drinks.
I love hearing about your weekend dinners,
And all those sights you still long to see.

I love talking family drama
And our unrealized dreams.
I love how you give everyone a chance,
No matter *how* bad they might seem.

I love your positivity, intelligence,
Laughter.
I love your beautiful heart,
Your unforced manner.

Most of all, though,
I love the way your soul shines.

Because I love all of you,
And ain't that the truth.
Touch this beating heart, this nourished soul,
And I promise you'll have your proof.

I love all of you—
I swear that's the truth.

Forbidden Fruit

In the city that never sleeps
There's a girl that still matters to me
Compassionate and smart, witty and sweet
The soul of an artist in a Midwest beauty

In the city that never sleeps
Taxi cars and crowded streets
Times Square and Broadway suites
All-night bodegas and so much cuisine

In the city that never sleeps
Ten million souls with ten million dreams
Light years away from the land of gold and green
Where I stand here wondering, if any of those dreams
Might still be for me

"Look, the Sun!"

I hold that last slow kiss in my mind—

Dawn's pale whisper
Peeking through the blinds.

I would've stayed there and kissed you forever—

For as long as those casino lights
Light up that desert.

Just two strangers kissing in the dark—

Folded hands
And unveiled hearts.

Imprint

Just for a moment
I tasted forever on your lips

Present-Day History

Our history started in History class:

There was only a foot or two between our desks—
Close enough that I could feel your breath.

I fell in love with you that semester—
Sharing gossip, takin' notes together.

You became the best part of my day, every day—
50 short minutes: It felt like winnin' the lottery.

A dozen hand-lotion fights, 100 conversations set to our own tune—
Twenty other students, yet we could've been the only ones left in that room.

My favorite distraction; the only school subject I wanted to learn—
The future would see you kissing my neck, letting your passion burn.

Back then, though, it was just you sitting next to me—
Our eyes drifting toward each other, even while writing.

Book Chaser

You said name a character after me.
I said, "Okay, who'd you wanna be?
The villain, the sidekick, the pauper,
The queen?"

You said, "I don't care.
Whoever she is, just make her words sing.

"Or, better yet,
Make her every action soar,
Until you got those readers of yours
Just *begging* for more.

"Oh, come on now, that won't be so hard.
What're you waiting for, a sign in the stars?"

Not that, I thought
But didn't have the courage to say.
But a sign that this actually means something,
That you're not, like always, just playin' games.

"Okay," I responded instead,
As I struggled to tamp my fears back down.
"Let me get to it, then,
And start working this thing out."

Jumpstart

We were in my car
When we kissed the first time.
Could've stayed right there forever, your lips locked with mine.

(Stars through the windshield,
The glass radiant in their shine.

Wind through the branches:
The only indicator of time.)

Just a kiss across the console—
Enough to bring me back to life.

Black and Green

I fell for you on beaches both black and green
I fell for you on that rec-room foldout, listening to the coquis sing

I fell for you on dirt roads and along rolling blacktops
I fell for you poolside and in quaint malasada shops

I fell for you in a kitchen decorated with strobe
I fell for you as we all danced along to some guy named Joe

I fell for you with your every sarcastic retort
I fell for you that time you laughed and called me a dork

I fell for you with every text and Snap
I fell for you as you begged me to just. come. back.

I fell for you almost beyond my control
I fell for you, babe, more than you'll ever know

First Date

I remember the clamor of that room
The voices, the laughter, the clatter of spoons
How none of it seemed to matter—
No, none of it ... except for me and you

Yeah, even then,
It was always just me and you

Black and Green

I fell for you on beaches both black and green
I fell for you on that rec-room foldout, listening to the coquis sing

I fell for you on dirt roads and along rolling blacktops
I fell for you poolside and in quaint malasada shops

I fell for you in a kitchen decorated with strobe
I fell for you as we all danced along to some guy named Joe

I fell for you with your every sarcastic retort
I fell for you that time you laughed and called me a dork

I fell for you with every text and Snap
I fell for you as you begged me to just. come. back.

I fell for you almost beyond my control
I fell for you, babe, more than you'll ever know

First Date

I remember the clamor of that room
The voices, the laughter, the clatter of spoons
How none of it seemed to matter—
No, none of it ... except for me and you

Yeah, even then,
It was always just me and you

Resort Living

You said you flirt by talkin' shit;
Felt myself flush
With every word you said.

I laughed along as you let me have it,
Just glad to be the target
You'd decided to pick.

Island Girl

You could've driven that thing with your eyes closed
Right at home with every swerve of the road
I glanced across the seat and you smiled at me
Backwards hat and cutoff jeans

I can still hear you singing along to those country songs
Beltin' 'em out, holdin' notes too long
You sat silent and simply listened on a few
As if all those words were written just for you

Well, this one—
This one's just for you:

You're my island girl
You're my salt-licked breeze
You're my all-day crush
You're my midnight dream

You're a patch of shade
In the summertime heat
You're the kiss of waves
Against two bare feet

You're my island girl
You're my all-time high
One glance my way
And I could've touched the sky

You're my island girl
And I hope you know:
I never meant to leave
Never wanted to go

You're my island girl
And I hope you see:
Even though I left
You're still here with me

Yeah, even though I left
You're always here with me

My mind always returns to that restaurant
Spent the whole night wonderin' if you liked me or not
You ordered pasta—pesto, if I'm remembering it right
Swirled it on your fork while I got lost in your eyes

I remember you telling me about your past, and about getting hurt
About new beginnings, and using what you've learned
About your fear of living life standing still:
Some deep-seated longing, desperate to be filled

Yeah, I hope you're still out there, girl,
Dreaming still

You're my island girl
You're my salt-licked breeze
You're the color to my eyes
You're the wobble to my knees

You're a patch of shade
In the summertime heat
You're a private beach
Beyond an ocean of trees

You're my island girl
You're my all-time high
A canopy of stars
Upon a canvas of night

You're my island girl
And I hope you know
Every moment with you:
All highs, no lows

You're my island girl
And I hope you see:
Never meant to cage ya
Just wanted you to be free

Yeah, even now, babe,
I'm prayin' that you're free

We stayed in touch for a month or two
But even then, I already knew:

You're my island girl, but you were never mine to keep
For even the strongest breakers are called back to sea

Yeah, even the strongest breakers
Wash out, eventually

You're my island girl
You're my salt-licked breeze
You're my all-day crush
You're my midnight dream

You're a patch of shade
In the summertime heat
You're the kiss of waves
Against two bare feet

You're my island girl
You're my all-time high
One glance my way
And I could've touched the sky

You're my island girl
And I hope you know:
I never meant to leave
Never wanted to go

You're my island girl
And I hope you see:
Even though I left
You're still here with me

Yeah, even though I left
You're always here with me

CORY KRUSE

Cliff Jumping

There are these cliffs in Hawaii
Where you can feel the ocean breathe;
Where the wind sings and dances,
And the waves wrestle and heave.

I jumped off that overhang trying to impress you,
Plunged feet-first into the cavernous deep.
Mustered all my courage to do so—
Had to shake off the trembling in both of my feet.

But when I finally surfaced,
I found you weren't even looking at me.
Your eyes were elsewhere: on the horizon,
And on some long-forgotten sea.

So I lowered my head,
Paddled back to shore,
And climbed out alone—
Dripping, shivering, sore.

I scrambled onto those rocks
Then slowly started my ascent,
Dodging wayward sea urchins,
And slurping ocean vents.

Even So

Fireflies live only
Eight weeks, they say
But how brightly do they burn
Even so

Worth It

"Let me buy you dinner sometime."

Across from me, you paused before responding, your freckles catching the sunlight like the spangled points of a constellation. Swallowing slowly, deliberately, you seemed to choose your words with great care, as one picks flowers, or browses a collection of expensive jewelry. "You know I'm leaving town soon, right?"

"Yeah, I know," I said. "Still ..."

You laughed, suddenly at ease, and shook your head. Still somewhat incredulous, you nevertheless allowed your cheeks to bloom into a smile, one more radiant than any of those constellations. "You're crazy. But all right, I'm in.

"Let's do it."

Quoth the Raven

Let's watch the sunrise on distance shores;
Let me feel my fingers wrapped in yours.
It's you I want, girl,
And nothing more.

Nothing more.

Castles and Moats

"This isn't an excuse,
But I just have to say:
I throw up walls whenever someone comes around—
I panic ... then run away.

"My mom and dad gave me trust issues,
The cynicism of love gone wrong.
Don't wanna relive that story;
I can't unhear that song."

"Walls, huh?" I said, still holding you close,
The two of us lying together, eye to eye
And nose to nose.

"Well, that's okay, because can't you see:
I ain't in no hurry; take all the time you need.

"You put up the walls,
And I'll just keep on climbing.

"I promise you that:
I won't stop climbing."

Old Friends

My sweet Jenny,
You set my heart on fire.
My sweet Jenny,
You're grace and light and pure desire.

My sweet Jenny,
You have me thankin' my lucky stars.
My sweet Jenny,
You got me believin' in Cupid's darts.

My sweet Jenny,
It's like our souls were old friends:
From the moment I met you,
Knew I had found love again.

My sweet Jenny,
Now you got me cursin' fate.
Oh Jenny, my Jenny,
Why'd you have to go away?

My sweet Jenny,
I know you're gone forever.
My sweet Jenny,
I'm fearing now I'll see you never.

My sweet, sweet Jenny,
Oh, I wish that you could see.
Oh Jenny, my Jenny:
Please come back to me.

Sequoia

You told me to stop listening so well,
When listening to you was all I wanted to do.
Who in their right mind would ever forget
Even the smallest detail regarding you?

You got a dog that looks like a lion
And a stormtrooper standing watch over your bed.
Your favorite food is a Portillo's hotdog
With ketchup and relish, in an even spread.

You take your coffee black
And your cocktails sweet.
Got piles of junk towering
In that Slug Bug's cramped backseat.

Your morning alarm is a rollercoaster ride,
One of the Hawaiian sort.
Whenever you get to laughing hard enough,
You always give this cute little half-snort.

Your soccer coach gave you a nickname,
One you haven't quite outlived.
Then there's Randy and Katie,
And your sister who teaches driver's ed.

You still get first-day jitters;
You worry about being seen.
Yet even now you dream of stardom
And lighting up the biggest screen.

I know one day I'll see you out there,
On the *Today Show* or something more,
Charming viewers with that smile, that golden laughter,
And dazzling 'em with your gorgeous heart.

When that day comes, I know I'll feel proud
And no shortage of happy, too.
'Cause here's the thing, girl:

No matter what happened between us,
I'll never wish anything,
Anything, but the best for you.

Golden Waves

I like to picture you down on the Florida coast somewhere,
With the sun-tossed wind
Dancing golden through your hair.

And with a congregation of disciples hanging onto your every word.
Not to mention the adoration of the fish, the sand,
The birds.

I like to imagine the palm trees bow to you along every beach-lined mile.
I know that the Sunshine State is brighter
With your each and every smile.

And that the ocean reflects your eyes of blue,
The waves prancing and twirling,
Performing just for you.

I like to dream myself back into your arms,
Lay there and feel the drum-song *thump, thump*
Of your sweet and lovely heart.

So often, then, I wish things were different.
That I was with you there,
Not back here, missin' it.

God,
How I wish things were different.

CORY KRUSE

"Distance Makes the Heart Fonder"

Our love is like the redwoods,
Rising tall, proud, and strong.
And old—yes, old too,
Surviving in a world in which they may no longer belong.

A sense of mystery courses through their midst—
A secrecy, a grandeur, a timelessness.

Tread those sylvan paths, and you'll soon get lost
In the stillness, in the splendor,
In the touch of infinity's kiss.

Tread those sylvan paths ...
And you will soon find your way
Back home.

Silence is not weakness; for,
Silent though they are,
Those redwoods endure.

They endure.

Haunted

I think about a lot of things,
But mostly I think of you.

All the days of my life ...
I know this to be true:

I'll be thinking of you.

CORY KRUSE

Rooftops and Boats

You're a picturesque beauty
You're a California queen

You're a cool breeze blowing
And the warmth of being *seen*

You're the best cheerleader
When you didn't have to be

You're a small-town girl
Who always wanted to leave

You're my favorite storyteller
And the best comic that I know

You're the one that got away
And still my every last-ditch hope

What If

It feels as if I've known you
All my life.

Now, wouldn't *that*
Have been the life.

Pony Express

Every message from you
Is like a correspondence from a long-lost friend—

And I fall in love again.

Thomas Rhett

For me, your memory's wrapped up in the radio
Summon you back with just a turn of the dial
Trading a broken heart for nostalgic smiles
Chasing your ghost over every windswept mile

And dammit—
I travel so many miles

You're the one song I can't bring myself to sing
A broken chorus, a halting melody
A grand piano with fraying strings
A scratched record just skip, skip, skipping

Yet you're a memory I can't afford to lose
Holdin' so tight to the mere echo of you
Miles apart—and worse things, too
But you'll always be the one,
The one I'd gladly choose

CORY KRUSE

You still flit across my mind when I hear that song
Two minutes, fifty-one seconds—wish it were twice as long
'Cause it still feels like we're together whenever it comes back on
And I can pretend there'll be a future for us, a *return* for your *gone*

But I know, deep down,
You've always been really, truly, gone

You're the one song I can't bring myself to sing
A broken chorus, a halting melody
A grand piano with fraying strings
A scratched record just skip, skip, skipping

Yet you're a memory I can't afford to lose
Holdin' so tight to the mere echo of you
Miles apart—and worse things, too
But you'll always be the one,
The one I'd gladly choose

GRACE IN THE DIRT

You and I were never meant to be
Obvious from the start, for everyone to see
Still, we were drawn together like tides on the sea
The two of us flowing as one, in perfect harmony

So, yeah, maybe we were never meant to be together
But we're still bound by an unshakeable tether:
Thick as steel, light as a feather—
And never one we'll completely sever

No, our love, girl,
Can never be severed

So now you're the song I can't help but sing
A beautiful chorus, a divine melody
A grand piano with flawless strings
A smooth record just spin, spin, spinning

And now you're a memory I'll always cling to
Just dancin' free in the afterglow of you
Miles apart—but no less true:
The girl of my dreams,
Whom I'll always choose

Yeah you're the one, babe—
The one I'll always choose

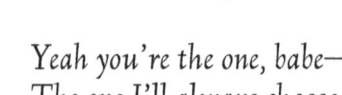

Stargazers

We were both on the roof,
Searching for something more.

Two hearts tied together,
Though our bodies were miles apart.

I peered off into the distance,
As though I might be able to find you there.

I settled for losing myself in the darkness, in the stars,
And trusting you, too, were giving them your stare.

We were both on the roof,
Searching for something more:

Neither of us able, at least right then,
To fully close that door.

Afterglow

Last night, I dreamed you came back to me.
Man, let me tell ya:
What a sight to see.

As beautiful as ever,
Euphoric and free.
And yet those ocean-blue eyes
Had eyes only for me.

We had all the time in the world
In that perfect dream.
I wrapped my arms around you
And listened to your heartbeat sing.

I kissed your forehead, your lips,
Your neck, your cheek.
Giggling, you pulled me in close
And did all the same for me.

All the time in the world ...
And yet, just like that, I woke bleary-eyed,
Without having had the chance
To say goodbye.

Left only with your afterglow,
I tried to clutch that dream in my mind ...
Then felt it inevitably slip away
Come first light.

Snapshot

That's how I'll remember you—
With sunlight filtering through your hair.

A golden crown, a halo,
And the promise of days ahead.

Out-of-Towner

I look forward to holidays, and not because of Christmas cheer.
But because I know there's an off chance
That you might just wind up here.

You got me scanning crowded bars,
Seeking out that freckled face.
I tell my friends, "Gonna do a lap,"
Before combing that whole damn place.

You got me looking at Insta stories,
Checking out all your friends' Facebook posts.
In a throng of familiar faces, it's *your* presence I yearn for the most.

When we do finally run into each other
It's like the world has fallen still.
You ask me how I'm doing;
I wonder just how much I should spill.

So instead I fall back on old platitudes
Before leading us to take some shots.
Side-by-side again with you,
I'm just grateful for my lot.

Out-of-towner, look at us here together.
Out-of-towner, could we somehow stay this way?

Because, the thing is—
You've always been my day-one crush,
And seeing you right now ...
Let me tell ya: It's the biggest rush.

So, Out-of-towner,
Tell me:
Will there ever be an *us*?

Can there be an us?

All It Takes

You make my night
Every time
Just by comin' around

One glance my way
With those speckled eyes
And I'm buzzin' for days on end

The In-Between

You like me when you're drunk,
Forget me when you're sober.
Can something that never started
Ever truly be over?

Paranormal Activity

I've fallen for a ghost,
Someone who isn't there at all.

I spend my days listening for bumps
And creaks in the night,

Holding out hope for a whisper,
A chill, a flickering of lights.

Hunting for some sort of sign—
Even just a hint—
That, in this large, drafty house,
I'm not the only one in it.

Maestro

There's a song that lives inside my head
Can't be stopped, can't be read

Sometimes it's sweet, sometimes it's blue
No matter what:
It's the melody of you

Daydream

I wanna hold you in the moonlight
I wanna dance among the stars
I wanna kiss you on the forehead
Hear you whisper, "I'm yours"

I wanna take you out to dinner
And laugh at all your stupid jokes
I wanna meet your mom, your dad, your brother
Write you a hundred thousand love notes

I wanna peer into your heart
And trace the sinews of your soul
I wanna know all of the little things
That make you feel warm, and bright, and whole

I wanna confess the way I feel
Wanna unscrew the valves on this heart
I wanna learn your every detail:
Every triumph, every fear, every scar

I wanna give to you my future
Invest my days in our love
I wanna treat you like the queen you are
Spend every second proving you're enough

In other words, darling, I want it all
I want it all

Longing

I'd give everything
For just one thing:
To hold your hand for a while

Haunted II

You got my head in a tangle
My heart in a vise
Not sure if this is torture
Or in some ways kinda nice

Can't lay my head on a pillow
Can't even shut my eyes
Without you appearing there before me
A loitering ghost in my mind

But if I have to be haunted
It's you whom I would choose
For there's no shame in your presence
No terror, when I'm with you

CORY KRUSE

The Revelations of Light

You're like motes of dust:
Visible during the daytime
But absent at night.

And even when you *are* visible—
What design guides your movement?
What purpose calls you to action?

Are you dancing, or merely
Drifting?

The Optimist

I've spent all these months
Tossing,
Turning,
Creeping—

Just hoping, of me
You've also been thinking.

Maybe you have;
Maybe it's just a fantasy.

Maybe I don't cross your mind at all;
Maybe I'm just another hometown fling.

Then again ... maybe I do.

Maybe I do.

Uncharted Waters

You made me a patient man.
Your silence, the distance,
Helped me to understand:

That love has no timelines,
No playbooks, no neat and tidy map.
That the heart spins on a different axis,
Its seasons not easily tracked.

You made me a patient man,
One waiting to discover
Just where your love might land.

The Plunge

If I told you how I feel,
Would it ruin it all?

Or does every love
Require a step to the edge,
    A plunge,
Some madman's desperate fall?

The Procrastinator

Someday
I'm gonna run out of somedays
So today I've decided to make today
The day

Please Stick Around

For so long, I've had this dam
Clogging up everything I feel.

But now—
Now I'm letting my cracks show;
I'm letting the waters run straight through,
Revealing all of me, to all of you.

Praying that such a flood
Will help you swim closer,

Not sweep you away,
Or simply drown you.

Armistice

I trundled out to no man's land
White flag wavin'
No weapons

And miracle
Of miracles:
You, too, ventured out ... and met me there

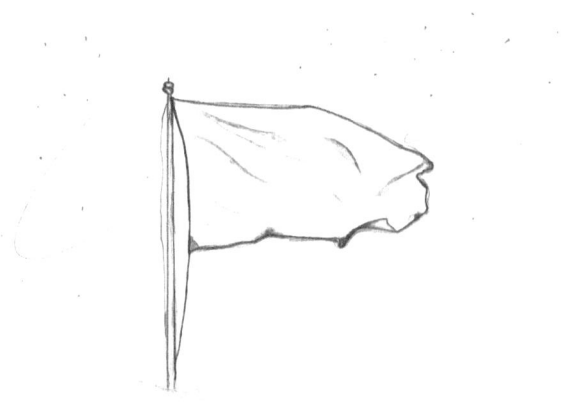

House Hunting

I found in your eyes
What I've always been searching for:

Home.

And a Thousand Moments Besides

We spent all of Thanksgiving break together;
It started with your friend carving snow angels in the street.
We laughed, got her up and got her home,
Then left to grab something to eat.

What followed were a dozen dinners
And a hundred episodes of *Planet Earth*.
Each night, I held you in the wintry darkness
And marveled at the way your lungs turned.

I remember that trolly with your grandma
And talking trips with your mom.
I remember going one-for-one with your grandpa
And dancing with your brother all night long.

I remember our first picture together
And that one with you in a dress.
Its diamond-sparkles had your skin a-glow,
And my heart in a soupy mess.

I remember that country concert
And the random lady who stole my drink.
I remember belting out those songs together,
Not giving a damn what others might think.

I remember every coffee date
And every minute of that Target run.
I remember buying toys for your dog
And debating which of them was the best one.

I remember going to the movies together
And every cheeseballs Netflix binge.
I remember talking faith, and God,
And all of our problems with religion.

I remember sending you flowers,
And how you went out of your way to get 'em.
I remember sitting and talking for hours
And knowing not even a hint of boredom.

I remember New Year's Eve
And how good it felt to have you by my side.
I remember that long, slow kiss
And popping champagne come midnight.

I remember it all—and a thousand moments besides.
I remember the way you sparked my heart into color
And brought meaning to my life.

I remember it all.
I remember it all.

Homework

I watched all of your favorite movies,
Memorized all your laugh-out-loud lines.
I listened to all those indie bands,
Even Rainbow Kitten Surprise.

I tuned in to your favorite podcast,
100 episodes and counting,
Anything to get to know ya better,
Even if I can't stand all that shouting.

I talked to your friends and family
Whenever we got separated at the bar.
I learned all of your silly nicknames,
Even that cheesy one for your car.

I soaked in every detail, every hobby,
Every preference, every fact.
Studied you like each moment was an opportunity
I wouldn't be getting back.

Yeah, I made a vocation out of learning you—
Hell, it's now my favorite thing to do.

A lifetime of study?
What a dream come true.

Locked In

A million distractions,
But you—
You're everything I need.

Your eyes so bright;
Your lips so sweet.

A hundred million distractions,
But you—
You're *everything* to me.

Chain-Link

To have you wrapped on my arm;
To have you wrapped on my arm:

The greatest of feelings,
The sweetest of charms.

To have you wrapped on my arm;
To have you wrapped on my arm:

A gift like no other,
A shelter from all harm.

To have you wrapped on my arm;
To have you wrapped on my arm:

Paradise in a person,
Safety from the storm.

To have you wrapped on my arm;
To have you wrapped on my arm.

Daydream II

I wanna sing a hundred songs with you
As we ride around in your car
I wanna just sit and talk for hours
And sketch patterns in the stars

I wanna tell you that I love you
And show you what that means
I wanna kiss you every morning
And meet your every breathless need

I wanna live this life beside you
And still have lives of our own
I wanna be your #1 biggest fan
And make sure you never go it alone

I wanna be your everything
And your one thing, and your best thing
I wanna be a piece and the whole
I wanna hold on, even while letting go

Dream Catcher

You're the girl of my dreams
And every dream I haven't yet dreamed

I / You / We

I got a fickle heart, but a lover's soul;
I yearn to hold on even while letting go.
I got restless feet, and wandering eyes,
But I froze in my tracks the moment you walked by.

You have a smile that could right the world.
You have a heart that could paint the sky.
Your laugh is the sweetest music,
And I can trace galaxies in your eyes.

We found our way together;
We found we were meant to be.
We found our best friend, our partner,
The answer to every Hail-Mary dream.

Isn't it incredible, my love,
How *I* and *You* became *We*?

Overthinking

I'm falling hard
I'm falling fast
Trying to find a way
To make this thing last

I'm running scared
I'm running blind
Wishing, more than anything,
That I could read your mind

I'm churning the waters
I'm muddying the scene
Flailing so hard
I might just ruin
Everything

Hills and Valleys

I know you better than anyone,
Yet I hardly know you at all.

Your every thought is a mystery;
Your heart, a valley wreathed in fog.

I want to charge through that wilderness,
Rush headlong into the haze.

But I'm always fearing that, if I do,
I might get lost along the way.

Cartography

Does the distance on a map
Determine the measure of your heart?

Do you love me because I'm close?
Would you still love me from afar?

Tethers

Is it love
That makes your fingers reach for mine?

Or only history
That keeps our hands entwined?

The Convenience of Love

Is it simply easier
For you to stay with me?

A familiar creature comfort,
Right there up with food, water,
And electricity?

Will you still be hanging around
When things aren't so easy?

Or will you be heading for the hills
And the next town over
That's bright and breezy?

Performance Art

You kiss me like you love me,
And I kiss you back,
Believing it fully.

You kiss me like we belong together,
But maybe, just maybe,
You are merely a good actor.

White Knuckles

I fear losing you
Every. Damn.
Day.

Overthinking II

I'm churning the waters
I'm muddying the scene
Flailing so hard
I might just ruin
Everything

But you—
You're as patient as ever
You're as cool as can be
Lending out grace for my failures
Love, for every misplaced anxiety

Medicine

Let time slip away
Let the days go by
Just hold me in your arms
And I know I'll be all right

Medicine II

The world's coming undone
But you
Hold my world together

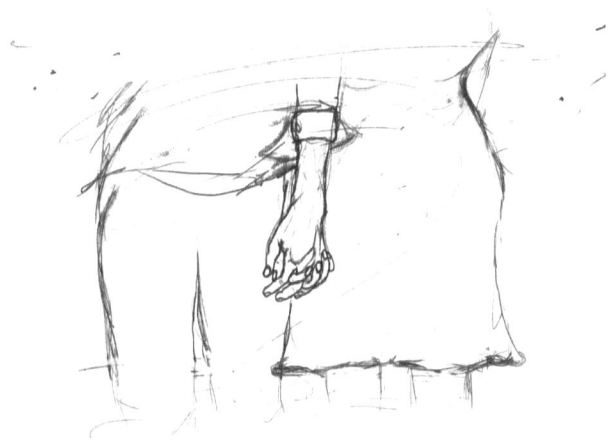

Hand-Holder

You're my hand-holder, getting me through the night
Drawing me closer and closer
Telling me it'll be all right

You're my hand-holder, on those days of rain
Keeping those coals a-smolder
Personally kindling the flames

You're my hand-holder, for every treacherous path
Traveling shoulder to shoulder
No reason to look back

You're my hand-holder, when the sun starts shining
Dancing with me
Along every silver lining

With you, my darling,
There's *always* a silver lining

The Great South Dakotan Baking Show

You had a meal kit you wanted to try,
One of those trendy, do-it-yourself kinds.
So you hauled over the ingredients and a bottle of wine,
And the two of us got to cooking late one night.

I asked you if the meal was spicy;
You said, "Oh, don't be a baby."
I laughed and shook my head.
You followed up and said, "Okay, maybe."

You made fun of me when I tried to chop an onion
And didn't have a clue.
Not to mention those avocados
And that stupid, misshapen spoon.

We shared that bottle of wine—
Then, later on, a second.
We watched a couple kids' movies:
Animated fare, which always gets ya laughin'.

I remember unraveling like the layers of that onion,
Bent out of shape like that old steel spoon.
I remember holding your hand in that screen-lit darkness
And wondering just what on earth I should do.

Maybe it felt like playing house.
Maybe it just felt right.
Maybe I was reading a future
Into what was only meant to last a night.

Maybe I enjoyed the idea of you and me together,
Sharing meals in perpetuity.
Or maybe I just liked how something so mundane
Could, with you, feel so extraordinary.

Elementary

I've tested your name with mine
Put together, they almost seem to rhyme

I've practiced that speech at least a dozen times
For when I'm down on one knee, watching that diamond shine

I've dreamt of all the days ahead: holidays and vacations
And every lazy Saturday spent in bed

Dancing in our kitchen, tailgating our kids' Little League
Holding ya on the couch
As you negotiate with a wayward strand of cheese

I've dreamt of a life spent with you—
I chuckle, knowing it a stupid thing to do

Still—
I've dreamt of a life with you

The Pledge of Allegiance

Call it a hoax, call it a lie
Call it delusion
Of the worst possible kind

Call it madness, label it a game
As crazy as it seems
I ain't going away

Call it foolhardy, declare it unwise
But I know what I feel, babe,
Right here on the inside:

I'm gonna love you
For the rest of my life

Dancing Partner

Love is what I feel for you
Love will I embrace
With your love I'll go on dancin'
Right down to my last day

Expiration Date

Everything has an expiration date
Everything—
Except what I feel for you

Expiration Date II

Deathbed—
Machines whirring;
Nurses scurrying;
Riddled with pain, through and through:

In that moment,
Right then,
My mind will be fixed on you.

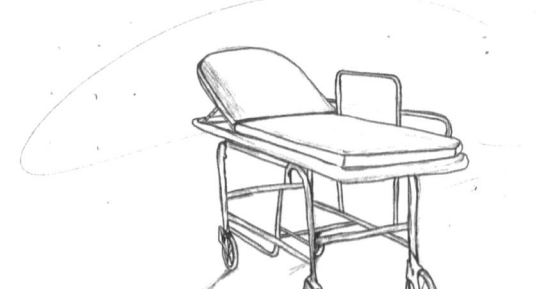

Love / Grace

Maybe love is less a feeling than a certainty,
A commitment to give to you
My everything.

Maybe it's the choice to choose you
Every day,
Unconditionally.

Well, if so,
Then that's a fate
I'd gladly choose for me.

Covenant

I've loved you from the first
I'll love you 'til the last
I love you, girl, no matter *what* comes to pass

Last the Night

I'll probably cry on our wedding day
Lose my mind when you turn my way
Tongue-tied, won't know what to say
Yeah, I'll probably cry on our wedding day

I might break down when I see those eyes
The spark of forever, a beauty from inside
I'll chase that gleam for the rest of my life
Yeah, I might break down when I see those eyes

I may just tremble when I hold you close
First-dance-spinnin', twirlin' on our toes
Hearts thumpin' while we put on a show
Yeah, I may just tremble when I hold you close

I'll probably grin as I kiss you deep
Skin shivering as you melt into me
Hearts tangled like those midnight sheets
Yeah, I'll probably grin as I kiss you deep

I know I'll love you all my life
Through every hiccup and every fight
Love strong enough to last the night
Yeah, I know I'll love you all my life

Vacationers

I want our lives to be like a honeymoon
Every moment, me and you

I want our tears to be only the happy kind
Saved for beauty, laughter,
And all the joyful times

I want our days to be one grand adventure
As we explore all that we can see
I want, too, for it to be a celebration:
Only the best kind of party

I want every day to feel like the first time
And the last time
With not a single moment gone to waste
I want to lose myself in our love, my darling,
And memorize every detail of your sun-soaked face

I want our lives to be like a honeymoon
Every moment, me and you:
Honeymoon

CORY KRUSE

The Problem with Forever

A million moments with you
Wouldn't be enough

A hundred thousand days
And I'd still be asking

For just ...

One ...

More.

The Artists

My head's in the clouds, my heart's in the stars
Living life beside you
Is the greatest of the arts

So grab the paint, and take my hand
Let's soak the canvas; let's coat this land

Let's create something beautiful
Something just for you and me
Let's plumb the depths of this ocean
And, in so doing, set ourselves free

All the Shadowed Places

If it's important to you
It's important to me

I wanna learn your heart
I wanna dream your dreams

So tell me it all, girl,
No matter how silly it may seem

Hold nothing back from your story:
No hope, no fear; no crack, no seam

Open yourself like a book …
And just let me read

Vacationers II

If leaving paradise is what it takes
To get to know all of you,

Then I'm ready, honey.
Pack the bags
Board the plane:

Let's go.

Vacationers III (or, Homebound)

The trip is over;
The honeymoon, gone.

The waves and palm trees have vanished;
The sunshine's moved on.

Aye, paradise has left us—
But not our desire to explore.

So let's keep learning each other every day, my love,
All of this—and so much more.

Heist

You're like a vault I don't have the combination to.
As much as I try,
I don't think I'll ever understand you.

Though ... the more I think about it,
The less I want to:

Give me the key,
But don't show me the lock.
Grease the hinges,
But don't spin the knob.

Let's keep the magic in motion.
Let's keep this adventure alive.
Let's peel the layers of this mystery
One beautiful ...

Step ...

At a time.

The Last and the First

Love: life's greatest adventure
And its simplest treasure.

Love: the purpose for it all.

LOSS

Or

The Lament of a Ravaged Field

*Heartbreak is a blight
That can creep its way
Into your very soul.*

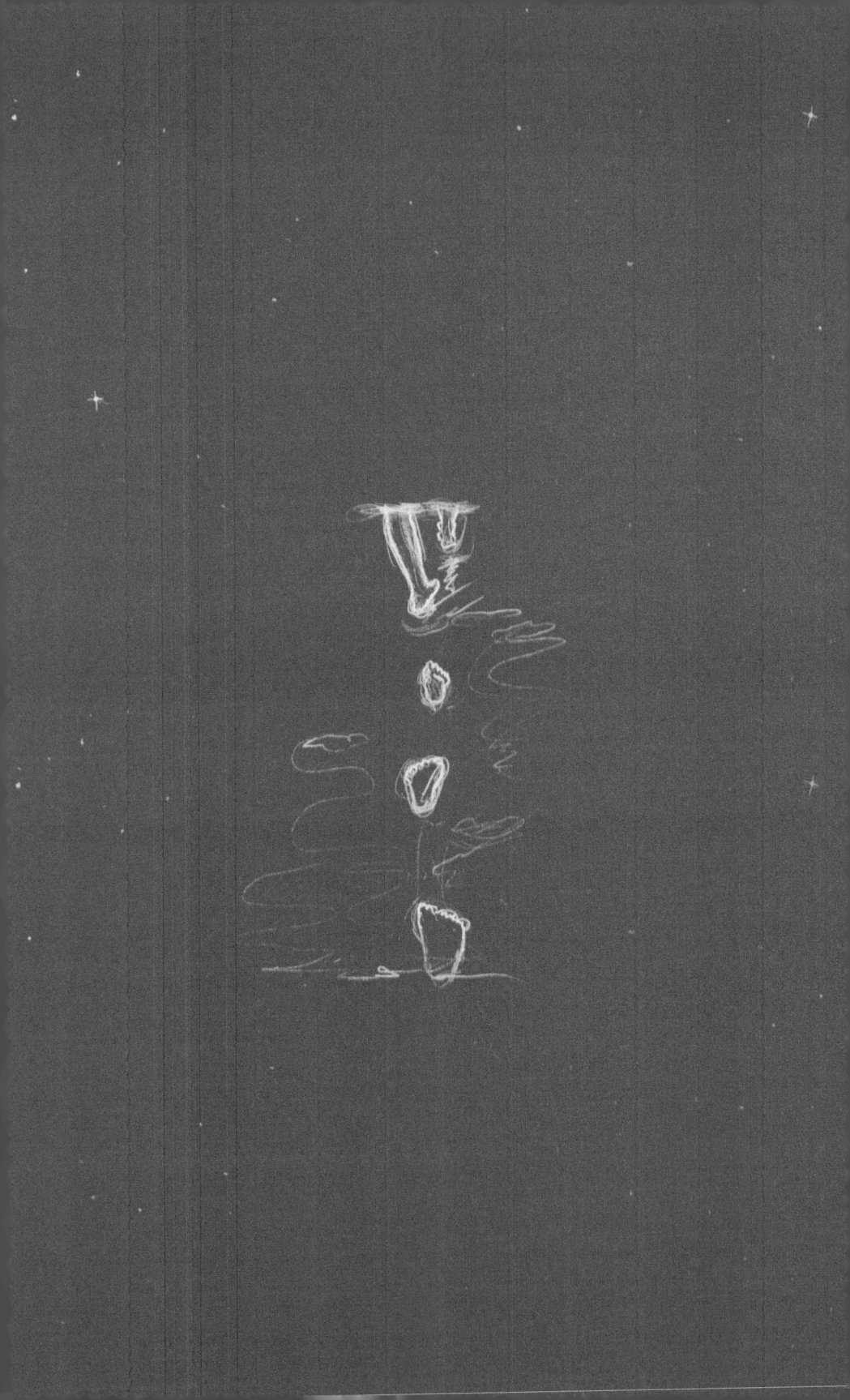

CORY KRUSE

Snapshot II

Whenever I picture you,
I see you with your back turned,
Walking away.

"I Gotta Hit the Road"

You were in a hurry that day,
That morning of the last time.
Somehow, I'd felt the end coming,
So I made sure to pause, and pull you in tight.

Lounging against my headboard,
I held you for a moment longer than I normally would.
You leaned your head against my chest
And damn, that felt good.

To just have the two of us
For another moment more.
No uncertainties, no bickering,
No beckoning doors.

Just two like souls sharing space in a silent room,
Time ceasing altogether
In the gray of that predawn gloom.

Just two like souls
Whose hearts were, just then, perfectly in tune.
But even in that moment, I understand now,
I'd already begun to lose you.

Yeah, I think somehow I always knew
That that morning was goodbye,
And that I'd never again get to hold you.

Today,

I'd give anything to go back to that moment
And squeeze you tight, just one more time.
To wrap my arms about you
In the stillness
Of that cold
February light.

Eulogy

I asked if this was goodbye;
You said, "Hardly."
Yet it felt like an end, the close to some party.

I asked if I would see you again;
You answered quickly, "Of course."
But there was a hesitation to your words, some fundamental lack of force.

Would I ever see you again?
Of course.

Yet here I am, all these days later,
Still waiting for that to be proven true.

God, I hope it's true.

Boomerang

Chase the dreams you need to chase,
Then please, oh please,
Find your way back to this place.

20/20

There's always a certain clarity
In every ending.

Ashes

And just like that, it was over
Realized I'll never again hold her
Nor see those stars shining
Like galaxies in her eyes

Just like that, it was over
Oh God, I should've told her
Now all I am left here with
Is goodbye

Postmortem

I'm still lookin' for a reason,
Still huntin' out a sign.
Still hoping it's a joke,
While dying on the inside.

Postmortem II

If you don't keep paddling—
Whether you're aware of it or not—
You're bound to drift.

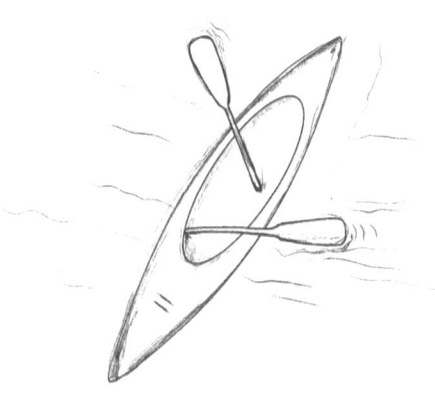

Postmortem III (or, A Picture Is Worth a Thousand Words)

You looked sad sitting next to him, with a shadow darkening your eyes
He didn't seem to notice, just kept trying to impress you with his best lines

Your legs were crossed neatly, your hands clasped together
Perched on that barroom stool, I'd never seen you unhappier

I should've been there beside you, not scrolling through my phone
I should've been enjoying that night alongside ya, not sitting at home alone

We should've been together; your smile shouldn't have been tucked away
We should've been arm-in-arm in that neon room, not 100 miles away

Dammit, I see that now:
We should have been together.

We should have been together.

Postmortem IV

I got lazy in my comfort;
I got jealous in my pride.
Assumed it was a sure thing—
Then cried out at the blindside.

Postmortem V

Did I ever get around to telling you I missed you?
If not, I swear I meant to.

Did I ever mention it's okay if we take things slow?
Because with you, I don't care *what* pace we go.

Did I ever say labels don't matter to me?
Because as long as we're together, I'm just plain happy.

Postmortem VI

You didn't ask
And I didn't tell
Now we're both living in this silent hell

You didn't call
And I didn't write
Now we're both sleeping alone at night

You didn't try
And I didn't understand
Now we're both drifting in this barren land

You didn't care
And I didn't move on
Now we're both still together ... and assuredly gone

Postmortem VII

By the end,
We were making inside jokes with other people,
Ones we didn't quite know how to share.

By the end,
We were making memories without each other,
Forgetting altogether the other wasn't there.

By the end:
A part and apart,
Conjoined souls ... and distant hearts.

By the end ...
The end.

Postmortem VIII

Was it poor timing that kept us apart?
Or some inherent deficiency
In both of our hearts?

Postmortem IX

I felt you pull away
Before you said anything at all.
Was it distance that sheared us apart,
Or was our love always destined to fall?

Maybe it was because you let go
Before I even started holding on.
Maybe there never *was* a happy ending for us,
No refrain to this song.

Maybe we just weren't meant to be;
I should have known that all along,
Probably.

Postmortem X

Yeah, maybe we were never meant to be;
Maybe this was always just some stupid pipe dream,
One dreamed up by me.

Postmortem XI (or, Quoth the Raven II)

Ours was a love built for distant shores.
Honeymoon hearts—
Maybe that, and nothing more.

Nothing more.

Postmortem XII

I would've married you,
But perhaps that was the problem:

What you needed from me
Was not what I needed from you.

The freedom I found in your arms,
To you, felt more like a cage:

My sense of belonging,
Your impulse to run;

My growing liberty,
Your lack of autonomy;

My radiant euphoria,
Your stifling claustrophobia.

Thus the closer I got,
The further you withdrew.
Every step nearer:
Two more away from you.

Postmortem XIII

I think about it like it was a special thing;
You think about it like it was just another thing.

I'd been online browsing, checkin' out rings;
Your attention was elsewhere, drawn to all the local kings.

I was planning a future, on hearing those wedding bells sing;
You were keeping your options open, a batch of lovers
Waiting in the wings.

Postmortem XIV

We were just two kids having fun;
Why'd I have to go
And think you were the one?

Postmortem XV

The stench of my insecurities
Must have gagged you.

Postmortem XVI

I was dating a ghost;
How hadn't I expected her to ghost me?

I fell in love with a stone;
How hadn't I expected her to be so cold?

I was drawn to an enigma;
How had I expected her to wear her heart on a sleeve?

Looking back,
I was aware of every red flag,
Yet I kept on, stubbornly.

Postmortem XVII

I saw it coming like an approaching storm
Yet I stayed outside, watching from the porch
Refusing to take shelter even as I felt unsure

Nor did I turn away as the wind buffeted me
And the dust stung at my eyes
Nor as the thunder growled overhead
And lightning carved up the sky

Never turning away, no—
Nothing as logical as that
Just kept on pigheadedly ...
Before the storm knocked me flat

Postmortem XVIII

I spent so much time polishing trophies
For someone who prefers
Ribbons

Postmortem XIX

You loved the idea of me
But don't you know
I'm not some painting or hanging thing

An appreciative eye is just that:
A burble of noise in a gallery
Momentary affection, then "On to the next"

You wanted the highs
Without any of the lows
You wanted star-crossed lovers
Without ever getting to know

You wanted the melodrama, the intrigue
You wanted the limelight
Without the drudgery

You wanted the glory
Without any of the studio sessions:
The uncertainty of early winter morns,
Where love is forged

Postmortem XX (or, Way Station)

Maybe I'm meant to love her
But not meant to be with her.
Maybe I was just a safe port
In the midst of a passing storm.

Maybe a harbor was never meant
To lay claim to a ship.
Maybe I was just one more stop
Along her life's passage.

A brief respite
Before she cast the sails,
Aimed the bow,
And sailed off toward distant shores.

Maybe I was always meant to be alone,
To be forgotten,
A lonely backwater whose only company
Is that roving lighthouse light.

(Or perhaps another ship will one day waltz in:
Bright sails tacking against the wind;
Navigating rocks and reefs
And seafaring barbarians.

Before finally reaching the harbor,
Where it'll fling its ropes,
Lower its sails,
And extend a gangway—

Where it'll finally anchor down,
With the intent to stay.)

Stockholm Syndrome

"Move on," they say—
As though it's a choice.

CORY KRUSE

Oleander (or, We Never Wanna Believe There's Poison Hidden in Pretty Things)

Who knew love
Could hurt this much.

Who knew its aftertaste
Held such a bitter sting.

Logic vs. Emotion

My mind understands the reasons; my heart
Understands
Nothing.

CORY KRUSE

Absences

Life without you
Is spring without flowers
It's a sunrise with no light

Life without you
Is a world devoid of color
It's snow in the midst of summertime

Life without you
Is a beach with no ocean
It's a forest stripped of its leaves

Life without you
Is a concert without music
It's a book set in a language you cannot read

Life without you
Is a wide-open horizon
And, somehow, still not feeling free

Life without you
Is no life at all
It's a world that's spinning—

                              Only spinning

Here to Stay

There are at least a dozen songs that remind me of you,
A bunch of movies,
Even a commercial or two.

There are a hundred things I couldn't get right,
But dammit, girl,
I swear I tried.

There are a thousand things I wish I could say,
But your heart's moved on,
And I know I'm too late.

Yeah, there are a thousand things I wish I could say,
But your heart's moved on,
And mine's here to stay.

Mine's here to stay.

The Watchman

One day, I hope you find what you're looking for
But this is all I am
And nothing more

One day, I hope you think of me
That when you look back
You remember fondly

The times we had
The good and bad
And the love that drew us together

One day,
If you ever find your way back

I'll be waiting
I'll be waiting

The Night's Watch

If I wallow in pain long enough,
In this fortress of my own making,
Maybe, just maybe,
She'll once more come a-calling.

If I simply refuse to abandon my post,
Perhaps my patience will be rewarded.
I'll see her come ridin' in, white flag in tow,
Up and over that horizon.

If that moment comes ...

I'll descend the wall;
I'll cast open the gates.
I'll rush out to meet her;
I'll kiss that freckled face

Until then ...

I'll keep my eyes on the horizon
And my heart in a vise:
Just cursing my misfortune
And chasin' shadows in the night.

"Long Live the King!"

There's a nobility in misery—
Or so I tell myself
As I am absolutely miserable.

With nobody around
To see just how good I am
At being regal.

Wasted Time?

Sometimes the hardest part about waiting
Is knowing whether or not we *should* be waiting.

Grasping for Straws

If I can just make you miss me,
Then maybe you will love me.

Bargaining

I'd dance a jig
Give the floor a lick
If only it'd make you smile

I'd spin a rhyme
At least a thousand times
If I could just hold your hand for a while

I'd give it all up
Every cent, every cup
If I could somehow draw you back

Because you, babe—
You're the best thing I ever had

The Muse

I put you in a book
As if that would make you stay.

As if that were enough
To express the entire universe
Etched into the canvas of my heart.

A single paragraph
To convey the wellspring of feeling
I had surging up on the inside:
An enormity,
An infinity,
All contained in a few well-placed lines.

You never finished that book, though,
And—who am I kidding—
You probably won't read this one either.

And yet ... the thing is,
All these stories—
I'm still writing them for you.

Peacocking

Spent all summer working out
Clean eating—nearly starved myself
Preparing for the day I'd see you on that lake ...

Joke's on me:
You never turned my way

Peacocking II

I'm Gatsby, chasing a green light.
Throwing celebrations
While dying on the inside.

I laugh with the rest of them.
I dance some manic, pathetic groove.
I slug back the bubbly
While hunting for your memory
In every bright, chandeliered room.

I entertain the others
While keeping eyes fixed across the pond,
Reflecting how, really,
You aren't so very far gone.

Not so far, no—
But always just out of reach.

So Close, Yet So Far

"I miss her so much."
What a stupid thing to say,

When, in reality, she's only a text
Or a Snap away.

Awake and Asleep / Asleep and Awake

I dreamed of you
In a hurricane
I dreamed of you
But you never came

I dreamed of you
On roads gone wrong
I dreamed of you
As I wrote this song

I dreamed of you
Like a shimmering mirage
I dreamed of you
And that last hug in your garage

I dreamed of you
And that Taco Bell date
I dreamed of you
And it felt like fate

I dream of you
Even during the day
I dream of you
When I'm wide awake

I dream of you
Because you are gone
I dream of you
Because I can't move on

Asleep and Awake / Awake and Asleep

I dreamed of finding you on a summer day
With the flowers in bloom and all the snow gone away

I dreamed of a hundred million stars shining in your eyes
Or perhaps it was just the gleam
Of all these fireflies

Eddies

The past lives within us like a thrumming current.
                      We can try to pull ourselves from its waters,

      But its undertow is too violent,
Its channel, too deep.

                    We can try to heave ourselves to shore—
                          Limbs flailing, lungs burning,

Driftwood-clutching—
      But that relentless river, that merciless maelstrom,

                Will always just drag us …
                      Right back.

It's Always the Little Things

All day I've burned with memories of you:

An inferno.

All day I've shivered with regrets:

I've never felt so cold.

Relics (or, Hairbrush)

Just one strand
That's all it was

A coiling twine
Of rich mahogany wood

Just one strand
A snag within those plastic teeth

Just one strand:
More than enough to level me

Relics II (or, Sweatshirt)

You still have a sweatshirt of mine.

I remember the morning I passed it your way:
Snow flurries in the air; the sky, a cold, slate gray.

I never asked about it at a later time,
Hoping it might, if only occasionally, bring me to mind.

As if a simple bundle of fabric
Could jumpstart a memory, or reignite a heart.
As if one hoodie could bind us together,
Keeping our love from tearing apart.

Yeah,
You still have that sweatshirt of mine.

Relics III (or, A Good Vintage)

You left a bottle of wine;
I still haven't popped that cork.

Can't bring myself to do it,
Not with its crimson contents seeming to jeer at me—
The fluid laced with not only alcohol,
But also with your memory.

Plus, they say wine only gets better with age—
A refinement through neglect.
So I guess I'll wait for that elusive day,
When it's as ripe as it can get.

You left a bottle of wine;
It collects dust in its rack.

Maybe I'll drink it on the day
When you finally come on back.

Broken Recollection

I wish I hadn't drunk so much;
I wish I could remember every word you said.

I wish I could relive those moments clearly—
A living record, stowed here in my head.

Mute

There's a particular sadness
That comes only from the words
Left unsaid.

The In-Laws

Your grandpa spoke to me like I belonged
Shared that homemade bottle 'til every
Last
Drop
Was gone

Thinking back, I'd have loved
To keep tagging along

You, me, and your family:
It never once felt wrong

Trivia Night

You have your phone set to military time.
There's a hitch in your breath when you sleep at night.
You talk to yourself on every big-city drive,
And sad commercials still make you cry.

You listen to bands only until they get famous,
Worried they will inevitably sell out.
You name your fish after Mexican food,
And your dancing could belong to a beached trout.

Your elbows bend at impossible angles,
And your knuckles crack far too easy.
You have no love for sugary desserts,
Would much rather have somethin' fried and cheesy.

You like *South Park* and *Star Wars*,
And any meme with dumb humor.
You feed your dog lunchmeat
And help our veterans hear clearer.

You once shut your finger in a car door
And bawled until they could pry it open.
Your dad was tough on you in softball,
But it got you in the paper, cheesin' and quotin'.

You have trouble opening up
And finding words for how you feel.
You show your heart through little gestures,
Every quiet glance over a homecooked meal.

Me? I have all this trivia
And a thousand little facts,
With no place to use 'em,
And no way to get you back.

Poison in the Balm

You gave me memories to last a lifetime.
Too bad it's *them* that kill me,
Every time.

Ballast

The more I drink you in
The more I sink.

With you,
There's no buoyancy.

Cruel and Unusual

You're like gum in the hair:

No matter what I try—

        Scissors, peanut butter, ice—

I can't be rid of you

        Without first making a mess.

Masochist

Do I love you
Or do I miss you?

Can these be one and the same?

Can we miss those things that destroy us?
Can we be addicted to the pain?

"Moving On"

It's difficult to close a door
When your own foot
Is being used as the doorstop

Cold War

Can't fight love with love
Nor fire with fire
Every twist of your knife
Springs forth more desire

Can't fight silence with silence
Nor grudge with grudge
Every vacant moment
Makes it harder to budge

This Doesn't Feel Like Home Anymore

I need a new city
I need a new town
Can't go anywhere lately
Without seeing you around

I need a new life
I need a new scene
Need somewhere safe
Where your memory can't find me

I need a new past
I need a new love
I'm looking for oblivion
When push comes to shove

Easier If

I wish I hated you.

Spiraling

If I were funnier—
Smarter—
Better looking—

If you'd opened up—
If I'd never caught feelings—

If we'd actually fought for once—
You see, I *wanted* you to fight with me

To exhibit even a little bit of passion for us
The fervor of joint ownership, of investment,
Of caring

Instead, all I got from you
Was always just
Apathy

Spiraling II (or, Who Wants to Be a Millionaire?)

Would you've loved me if I had a million dollars,
Or only if I had a million more?

Would you've glanced my way if my face was another's,
Or have still turned and walked out that door?

Spiraling III (or, Inadequacies)

I would have loved you with all my heart.
Maybe that wasn't enough.

Maybe I wasn't enough—
Not enough to make you stay.
Not enough ... in every single way.

Spiraling IV (or, Who Will Ever Stay?)

What if
I'll never be good enough?

What if
I simply wasn't made for the long haul?

Spiraling V (or, Self-Talk)

Once you're perfect,
Then you'll find the one,
Or so goes the voice in my head.

Once you're finally put together,
Someone might actually love you.
So, you best be gettin' on about gettin' better.

I hate that little voice, that whisper, that *scream* ...
And yet I can't bring myself to tell it that it's wrong.

Make yourself lovable enough, it carries on,
Or I promise you'll end up alone.

Spiraling VI (or, Chasing the Wind)

I'm a fool for thinking I had a chance with you;
But I suppose only a fool wouldn't have tried.

You are the Sorcerer's Stone.
You are El Dorado.
You're an undiscovered country
And the promise of tomorrow.

You're Pandora's Box.
You're Murphy's Law.
You're the draw toward fire
And every silver-tongued siren's
Ensnaring call.

You're the Fountain of Youth.
You're a quest with no end.
You're the world's greatest cipher
And a long-lost friend.

If, indeed, you are all of this,
Who then, I ask, could ever resist?

Spiraling VII (or, The Fool and His Fancies)

Maybe I should have been meaner.
Maybe I should have been cold.
Maybe I should've kissed that stranger
That night there on the boat.

Maybe none of it matters;
Maybe none of it ever did.
Maybe I was just a fool—
Who am I to kid?

Spiraling VIII (or, Old Habits Die Hard)

You still loved him,
Didn't you?

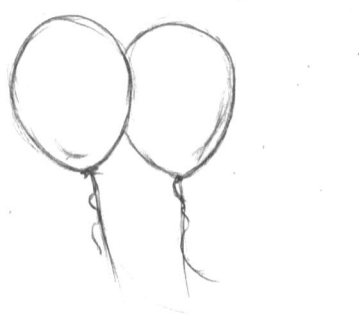

Spiraling IX (or, Your Future Husband)

I got one night;
He'll get the rest of your life.

CORY KRUSE

Spiraling X (or, Different than Mine)

When you said goodbye for the last time,
I thought, *Thanks a lot for wasting my time.*
But if all of that was just wasted time,
Then why is every moment still seared in my mind?

And now I'm left here wondering,
Do you ever still think of me?
Or was this just an on-again, off-again sort of thing?

And does the memory of us lying together
Still take your breath away?
Or, for you, was that just any ol' day?

Do you ever dream of the grooves on my face?
Do you ever long to reach for my hand?
Or have you already cast off your feelings
And slammed the door on this also-ran?

Lying here with my fingers tingling and cold
—Your memory like a shrine—
I'm beginning to fear your answer
Is much different than mine.

Diverging Paths

You got better, while I got worse
Chasing blessings, while I stayed cursed

You moved on, while I stayed planted
Searching out love, while I found sadness

Yeah, all there is left now
Is sadness

Grasping for Straws II

For a time, I wished I could make you jealous,
Wished I could make you care.
But now I've come to realize:

Neither was enough
To bring you back here.

Because I ain't nothing to you but a memory,
Someone who helped stave off the lonely,
Even if it was only just temporary:

I ain't nothing to you
But a memory.

Operator

I'm waiting for a call
That's not coming

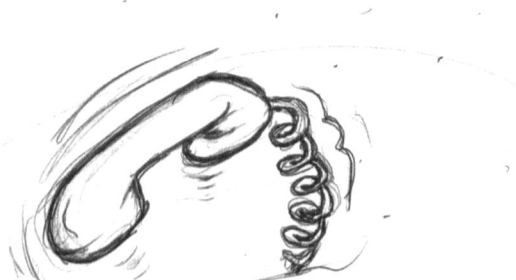

CORY KRUSE

Wanderers

It was a long time ago, in a land far away
Could've reached out to you
But I had nothing left to say

'Cause you ain't comin' back
And I ain't comin' home
This world now is nothin'
Nothin' that we used to know

Yeah, you ain't comin' back
And I ain't comin' home
The people we thought we were
Died out on their own—

Died together, all alone

Mirage

It's a shadow,
What we once were.

I reach for it,
Expecting purchase,
Expecting something—anything—

But my fingers find only ...
Empty air.

Hyperbole

"I'll always love you."
What a thing to say.

Water Vapor

You're a plume of steam:

No substance,
All hot air.

Even Now

I thought I loved you;
I was wrong.
Now you're just some girl
I'm wasting words on in a song.

I thought I knew you;
How could I have been so wrong?
I knew only what you showed me,
A graffitied façade covered in smog.

I thought this was forever;
My timekeeping has never been so off.
You were my future;
I was just another boy who'd gone soft.

I thought I could move on;
I haven't yet discovered how.
Because seeing you out
Still makes me seize up, and ache, even now.

Even now.

Me to Me

Open your eyes:
This thing was broken from the start.

Signposts

I asked for the truth
And maybe just a little bit of effort
But you continued down the path of least resistance

I asked for honesty
But you kept on spinning riddles
Like the troll under a bridge

I asked for a hint, a clue
But you merely cackled at my expense
Smug, you rubbed your reptilian hands together
While hopping from limb to limb

And that's the moment I knew
That it'd always been worthless
Loving you

Clear Eyes

You were an enigma I was determined to crack;
Made a fool out of myself trying to make ya laugh.
Now I feel like double the fool whenever I look back:

What had I possibly seen
In a heart like that?

Masquerader

You're poison
Wrapped up in a pretty face

You're a riptide
Beneath docile waves

You're prison walls
Behind welcoming gates

You're stern judgment
Within a sympathetic gaze

You're a beckoning mirage
Where there's no water at all

You're an offered number
With no intention to call

You're a pinky promise
Without a hint of follow-through

You're sun-scorched pavement
With no socks, no sandals, no shoes

You're a fireworks finale
That turns out to be a dud

You're a conscientious objector
Holding tight to a smoking gun

Celestial Beings

You're like a comet:
Beautiful from a distance
But, up close,
Little more than space trash.

Okay, okay,
I didn't actually mean that.
I just wish there was a way
I could hurt you the way you hurt me.

Because your leaving
Was like a black hole—yanking,
Swallowing,
Eradicating.

And now your memory
Pulls me like gravity—
But too much of it—
Keeping me anchored
And going nowhere at all.

You Made Me Feel So Small

You kept your options open like a buffet line
A roster of lovers just waiting on the side
I was the weekly special, discounted that night
You merely glanced at the chalkboard
As you sauntered on by

You snapped those steel tongs
Beneath each of those buzzing heat lamps
You tried every one of those grease-soaked dishes
Before simply doing another lap

Meanwhile, there at the host's stand,
I stood shadowed and forgotten,
Realizing, finally,
That you weren't at all interested.

Witch's Brew

It swirled and bubbled and steamed
That poison you proffered to me

Yet I drank it up
Every time you passed that cup—
Anything to not upset the balance

Yeah, I guzzled it down to its last drop
Because, in the end, I trusted you—
And what a stupid thing to do

Or so I realized as I choked
And writhed
And felt the bulge of pressure
Expanding in my eyes—

Or so I realized
As, with a wicked smile,
You sat and watched me die

Sherlock Holmes

You cheated on me on a Monday
Couple drinks with your classmates
Pitcher races at a local place
Turns my gut when I picture your face

You disappeared even on weekdays
Gone for hours, showin' up late
"Dead phone," asleep at your place
I'm a fool for believing the things you would say

Your games had me doubting *everything*
No proof, but always second-guessing
Feelin' paranoid, yet stomach twisting
Begging for answers with none forthcoming

You finally broke my heart on—get this—a Monday
Sudden silence, left me out to wait
Through text, you delivered my fate
Too numb, then, to even rustle my hate

So I guess I'm a world-class detective
And apparently an utter fool
Knew just what was happening behind my back
Yet I kept on like some desperate tool

Hurray, I'm a world-class detective—
But one who knows nothing at all
Because even now I'm sitting by my phone
Just waiting for you to call

Dammit, I'm always waiting for your call

The Hunter

You gutted me like a hunter
Does a deer:

Strung me up,
Twisted your knife;
Scraped me out,
Discarded the insides.

You shot me dead, and only for sport.
Not out of necessity
Or as some reluctant last resort.

So now I'm a pile of steaming entrails
Left forgotten in the brush:
Caked in leaves and blood
And so many memories of us.

Yes, our love is just another trophy
You never look at anymore,
One propped up against the wall
In some poorly lit backroom—

Collecting dust in the shadows,
And cobwebs in the gloom.

Paper Shredder

You're not what I needed;
You tore me into pieces.

I can still hardly believe it.
One day, I hope you finally see it:

You tore me into pieces.

The Choices You Made to Lose Me

You lie to your friends about how it all went down:

Turned yourself into a martyr,
And me into a clown.

You never take an ounce of responsibility:

Eight years of neglect,
And somehow it's still *me* who ruined things.

You played oh so many games:

A manipulator adept
At making me remember her name.

You called me up only when you were lonely:

Just broke up with your boyfriend—
"Come over and hold me."

You kept me around as a backup plan:

It's like you loved the power you held,
Not holding my hand.

You made every conversation about you:

Always happy to listen,
But would've been nice to get a question or two.

You cheated on me at least a couple times:

But we were only *talking* then,
So, "Not a big deal; it's fine."

You always say that you still love me:

Drunken words that end up meaning
Nothing.

Whenever You Show Up

Don't mistake my body's jolt at seeing you
As excitement.

It's just my instinctual fight-or-flight,
A natural aversion to the stovetop
That once burned me.

#Cringe

You ain't nothin' but a memory, and I ain't nothin' but a fool
Your departure left me hollowed out
Your silence, like the worst kind of tool

Now I'm ashamed of my emotions
I regret that I ever cared
I never should've given up so much
All those little pieces of me that I shared

I'm embarrassed for loving you, and now ain't that just sad
Because love should be a badge of honor
Not something you wish you could take back

Chameleon

I became who I thought
She thought I was.

Hoop Jumping

I almost went broke trying to impress you
Bought all the nicest clothes and all the best shoes
Snagged those concert tickets and that hotel suite
Another swiped card didn't matter to me

I almost went deaf listening to the music you like
Anything, to a snag a glimpse inside
Headphones popped in every other night
Maggie Rogers still crooning come first light

I almost went mad trying to understand you
A bag of mixed signals and impossible clues
An exercise in futility: a vault no one has the key to
Yet a brick wall I was still desperate to woo

I almost grew old waiting for some effort
Even just a morsel more, to me, would've mattered
But your affections remained distant,

                Scattered

And now my heart remains in shreds:

                        Frayed, tattered

"You've Changed"

I sacrificed myself on the altar of love
Gave up who I was
Just trying to be enough

Twisting and turning
And jumping through hoops
Slamming doors behind me
Joining up with new groups

Yeah, I sacrificed myself on the altar of love
Gave up who I was
Just trying to be enough

And now I have a stranger looking back in the mirror
All for someone
Who's no longer here

CORY KRUSE

The Compounding Effects of an Obsessive Mind

I missed so many moments
Waiting around for texts that weren't comin'

Phone in my pocket, phantom buzzin'
Checking it like an addict, mind always runnin'

Fearing I was missing a moment with you
When it was the people around me
I should've been devoted to

So I wouldn't end up losing them
As I was already losing you

The Skeptic

You made a cynic out of me.
Your love—
It tainted everything.

Even now, I feel your shadow lurking.
Your ghost—always tugging,
Grasping at my hands, my ears, my knees.

It's in all of my conversations;
It plagues my every Saturday night.
I find it prowling, even,
As I peer into a stranger's eyes.

You made a cynic out of me:
Haunted, hollowed out,
Trusting nothing.

A cynic,
Suspicious of life itself.

CORY KRUSE

"Moving On" II

I love in her
All the things
That remind me of you

Misery Loves Company

Maybe we don't love each other
Maybe you're just damaged
In the same way as me

Pawn Shop

I'm just a number you can call when you're lonely;
Always feel a distance
Anytime you hold me.

But I guess all of that is to be expected;
It's just the way of the world anymore:

An Earth full of strangers,
All using each other
In a hopeless quest for pearls.

Games II

We skim the surface
We chase the ride
We win the battle
But lose the fight

Games III

We're both playing the game,
But there are no winners here:

Everyone's playing
By their own set of rules.

Ceasefire

(Even now
I'm trying to make you love me
Even now
Just trying to make you see

Even now—
Despite everything—
I know we're meant to be)

Back at It

I'm just another drop in the bucket,
Just one more Snap on that phone in your pocket.
Just one more choice on a long-line,
Deep-fried, discount love buffet ...

... and you never turn my way.

Commitment-Phobe

Everyone's always changing their minds at random,
With scarcely an explanation given.

Lyin'...
Cheatin'...
Ghostin'...

And leaving me on READ:

Countless little games—
All designed to mess with my head.

"Just Wait 'Til You See the View"

It's all my fault:

I threw the rope;
I climbed the walls.

Who can I blame, then,
When I lose my grip ... and inevitably fall?

Wedding Season

I thought I'd done everything right:
Kid's table, laughing together all night;
Takin' selfies, slow-dancing in the strobe lights;
Haunted house tours, and karaoke rides.

Yet none of it mattered:
Like all the others, when the time came,
You merely cast me aside.

Wedding Season II

The death stroke came out of left field:
A perfect day, a promising night,
Everything going so well ...

Then, well, all of it went straight to hell.

No rhyme, no reason, no moment to blame.
Watched you leave with somebody else
And knew it'd never be the same.

It's not even the heartbreak that gets to me;
It's the lack of closure, the randomness,
The uncertainty.

The never knowing why:
A lifetime of wondering
With no answers in sight.

Oleander II

Would I still have taken a bite
If I knew the outcome?

(Probably.)

We never wanna believe there's poison
Hidden in pretty things.

Just One More Time

Every good sin
Deserves to be tried twice.

Exit Strategy

You got me swipin'
Before I even arrive on the scene:

Gotta have a plan in place
For when you inevitably leave.

Another One Bites the Dust

Do what you gotta do;
I'm used to this pain.

Hell, I've *trained* for it.

Pyro

"Moving on" has had the same effect on me
As throwing water on a grease fire:

The flames just get higher and higher.

(But maybe a part of me *wants* to burn it all down ...
So come on, let's add some more water.)

Through the Night

I'm looking for love in all the wrong places
Clawing around in shadowed spaces
Desperate for belonging in strangers' faces
Yeah, I'm looking for love in all the wrong places

I'm breaking hearts in my quest for healing
Loneliness, my motive for stealing
Selfish actions; leaving others reeling
Yeah, I'm breaking hearts in my quest for healing

I'm giving up myself for a chance at connection
Trading who I was, throwing away my conviction
Abandoning truth for the guise of perfection
Yeah, I'm giving up myself for a chance at connection

I'm finding myself lonelier than ever
Starting to doubt this will ever get better
Wondering if I might just stay numb forever
Yeah, I'm finding myself lonelier than ever

Belly Up

It was a long day of sober thinking
So it's gonna be a long night of no-holds drinking
Into an ocean of booze I'd rather be sinking
Than the oasis of your memory
Which will only sink me

If I can forget for a while, then sign me up
Keep pouring fiery medicine into this barroom cup
If I can lose myself in the swirling neon lights
Then maybe, just maybe,
I'll make it through the night

Plus, I need that weeping glass to keep my fingers distracted
The very same function as any straight jacket
Keeps me from caving and outright crackin'
Reaching for my phone
And hammerin' out some lovesick message

Not to mention I crave that old-timey music
And the company of that old popcorn machine
At least there's no trace of you in those salted kernels
No buried memory in its oily sheen

At least here I'm alone but not alone
And, who knows, maybe I'll catch a stranger's eye
At least here, in the semidarkness, I can convince myself
That everything
Is gonna be just fine

"Rough Night?"

Nights so rough
My Face ID
Don't recognize me

Can't calm these thoughts
Can't catch no sleep

Nights so rough
They follow me into the day
Where I'm stuck with what I've done
All those stupid things I say

Nights so rough
And mornings of gray
Just laying there in agony
Wishing I could drink it away

Soon enough, I know
I'll drink it away

The Shallows

I starve myself to prove my worth,
Yet I still can't snag a second glance from her.

I change my hair, my teeth,
My shirt:
Yet I'm as numb as ever
And no closer to the cure.

I bend myself double doing core,
A thousand sit-ups
Then ten thousand more.

Not even sure what all this is for:
Just another sculpted body
You're bound to ignore.

I've dredge up my soul,
Threw my treasures to shore.
Loitering in the shallows,
But so desperate for more.

I'm always so desperate
For so much more.

The Shallows II

Yeah, I dredged out my soul
Sacrificed authenticity
Thinking it'd make me whole

Dimmed my inner light to go chasing after ghosts
Splashed around in the shallows—
While forgetting my way home

The Shallows III

I chase after shiny objects,
All for the chance to belong.

The thing about shiny objects?
They often don't *want* to be caught.

The Shallows IV

You can still drown
In shallow water.

The Shallows V

I thought you were what I needed
Turns out, you were just conceited

Now I'm packin' my bags
And surely leavin'

Gonna go find somethin'
I can believe in

Insanity Is Doing the Same Thing Over and Over and Expecting a Different Result

I keep returning
To the things that hurt me

Repentance

It's time to turn this sinking ship around
It's time to lay this tattered body down

It's time to stop chasing
After every glittering storm

It's time to find sanctuary, at last,
Within my own home port

It's time to seek harmony
Instead of raging seas

Peace, rather than the thrill
Of churning waves

Which always
         Wreck me

20 Seconds

Dirty hands
Require more than just soap and water
To get clean:

They need to be scrubbed.

Purgatory

Patience is a poison.

I guzzle it
　　desperately.

Dissociation

It's funny how, with time,
Some memories begin to feel
Like somebody else's story.

New Perspective

Time doesn't so much heal
As swap the lens.

Salvation in Oblivion

I meant nothing to you
But maybe that's okay
Maybe feeling like nothing
Was the one thing that'd get me to walk away

Maybe feeling like nothing
Was, in the end, the very thing
That *saved* me

Paintbrush

We're a swirl of memories
We're a collage of lives
We're a jumbled melting pot
Rolling on the inside

We're all things
And most things
We're some things
And no things

We're bad bets
And sure things
We're long days
And learned things

We're all the people
Who aren't us
Those who inspired
And loved and hurt us

Yeah, we got the colors of others
Mixed in our paintbrush

And so we paint ...

Locksmith

Acceptance is the key
That unlocks the path to healing

Old Habits (or, The Deliberations of a Wandering Mind)

Maybe I was nothing to you,
But you were everything to me.

(Would've bought you a house;
Would've got down on one knee.)

Sometimes, I still wonder
Are ya ever still wondering
About me?

Or am I now all but forgotten—
Just the echo
Of some distant memory?

Old Wounds

Seeing your name still stops my heart cold.
Your picture? A dagger to the soul.

Permafrost

Am I destined to always feel this way?
Or will the heartbreak, one day,
Up and fade away?

Right now, I can't be sure.
Though, Nature has shown me that
Even the sharpest icicles
Eventually melt down,
Into puddles.

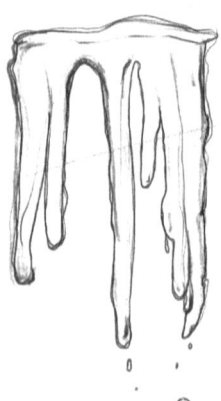

Sad but True

I still look back at our texts sometimes,
Just to see if there was some way I could've made things right.

I still go out hoping I'll run into you at the bars;
Even at the lake, I'm huntin' for those soft freckles of yours.

I can't drive by without at least glancing at your house.
Always wondering if you might be home,
Or if there's a chance I'll see ya out.

I still wave at your parents on my morning runs;
It always puts ya front and center,
The memories badgering me until I'm done.

And I once stumbled across your picture gracing the yearbook line;
Up until then, I had told myself I was perfectly fine.

In fact, I can't even see an ear without thinking of you:
A thousand little things determined to cloud my view.

Trust me, I realize it too.
Could I be more pathetic, less capable of reading the room?

I know, I know: It's sad, but true.
Because most of all, girl, I'm still in love with you.

Yeah, there's no denying this truth:
Darling, I'm still in love with you.

The Martyr

There's no end in sight for me:

Still, despite it all,
I love you earnestly.

I love you earnestly.

Voyager

I dream of an unbroken horizon,
And the courage to track her down.

DESPAIR

Or

The Ache of a Fallow Soul

The ashes of a broken life cry out;
But who is there to answer?

CORY KRUSE

The Human Condition

Tragedy stalks our days
Like a shadow.

Inevitably, then,
We learn to avoid the sun.

Landslides and Hurricanes

Destruction comes—

    sweeping,

        unbidden,

            cruel.

Remorseless,

    it darkens the sky;

        gluttonous,

            it snuffs out all available light.

Trust is shaken;

    memories are soured;

        hope is crushed.

Until dreams,

    plans,

        affections,

            friends,

                are reduced to little more than lonely ashes

    drifting aimless

        upon the wind.

We Interrupt This Program

It's impossible.
It's not true.

There's no way this world
Could extinguish such a light,
Not one as bright as you.

...

Oh God, *please* God,
Let it not be true.

Fake News

Everybody blathers about fake news; why can't this be that?
Is it really so inconceivable
That someone has misconstrued the facts?

I mean ... we'd just talked last week,
Something dumb, as normal as can be.
There's no way, then—right?—
That this can be reality.

There's no way you're not still down there,
Just drinking up the sunshine.
There's no way all that's left of you now
Is this wisp of memory in my mind.

There's no way; there's simply no way.

Fact-Checkin'

You can't be gone—
No, not you.
Your heart is a universe in motion;
Your soul, the most vibrant of hues.

No, you can't be gone.
Not you.

"My Condolences"

There were all those texts from friends
To which I didn't know how to respond.
It's not like we were still together;
You had long since moved on.

Likewise, in moments like this,
What even *is* there to say?
What are the proper words?
What sentiments could fix this day?

And truth is, I'm not sure I even know *how* to grieve.
All I crave is silence, isolation: a nothingness
To fill up this emptiness
Lodged here inside of me.

Shell-Shocked

I couldn't process the news when first I heard
Grew number and number with their every word
I hit the floor like a wing-clipped bird
Just gaped at my phone and felt the Earth turn

I managed to crawl myself to bed, eventually
Just sat alone in the dark, emptily
Couldn't put to words the storm raging inside of me
Thought instead of caged dogs and all those wasted dreams

Neither could I summon tears; not then and not now
Just this stretching silence, this puckered brow
Can't help feeling I've somehow let you down:
Too many smiles, not enough frowns

Nor could I believe it; still can't to this day
I'm convinced, even now, that it might be some mistake
Because I was always told life wouldn't go this way
And 'cause you're the kind of person we were meant to celebrate

    Not one whose memory

        Would just fade away ...

Investigative Reporter

I read every article.

I scrolled every feed, every timeline, every Snap.

I wore my retinas raw,
As if that would somehow bring you back.

I tried to make the news sink in.

I was desperate for the horror of it
To finally click.

I needed to feel something, anything,
Not just this numbing, cowardly sick.

Soundbites

They said it was an accident.
They said it happened fast.
They said they rushed you to the hospital;
They said you're not comin' back.

Yeah, I understand that now:
You're never coming back.

Culpability

I could blame Florida
I could blame the motorcycle
I could blame that winding road

I could blame that tree
The guy you were with
You, for ever leaving home

I could blame myself
—and Lord knows I do—
Between accusations at the TV
The media
The news

I could blame God
I could blame the devil
Fate, bad luck,
Or circumstance

Hell, I could blame the whole world ten times over
And it still won't be enough to change the facts

Ten thousand leveled fingers—
But you are still not coming back

Complicity

It may be worthless,
But I still have to blame something,
Or someone.

Because if I don't
That means you died for nothing,
All alone.

Enabler

Another light gone out;
It's like the world is determined
To plunge us all into darkness.

Why is it
That the dark is permitted
To extinguish such radiant lights?

How come life's default setting
Seems to be set
To tragedy?

I ask you:
Where is the sheriff?
Where is the shepherd?
Where's the keeper of the keys?

What emergency drew your attentions elsewhere?
What boredom lulled you to sleep?

Where were your eyes,
Your hands,
Your heart,
Your feet?

Where were you
When you had somewhere critical to be?

Where *were* you?

Opening Remarks

Answers are good;
Justice is better.
But I'm not sure either
Are enough to make me less bitter.

They're poor restitutions
For wanton negligence.
They're a pity offering
For putting us through this.

They are everything,
And they are nothing:

A hand full of sand
Squeezed tight,
With nothing else to cling to.

Cross-Examination

What good is blame
Or answers
Or closure

What rationalization
Could explain away
The dousing of your light

No, maybe sometimes things just happen
Maybe there *is* no grand design

Maybe all of this
Was always just
Random chemistry in the night

Maybe it's always just been pure
Unbiased chance

To which I say:
The hell with that

CORY KRUSE

The Prosecution Rests Its Case

I ask again: What good are answers

What justification
Could possibly make this make sense

What excuse is there
What reasoning would ever suffice

I know now all of that is bullshit
Because there *are* no answers in this life

Verdict

Meaning is scarce;
Chaos is rampant.

We're lost in the folds
With no way to tamp it.

Closure is a lie;
Healing is a phantom.

Fairness is a falsehood,
Bound to some tactless deity's
Latest tantrum.

CORY KRUSE

Bargaining

I'd give it all up
If you'd somehow gotten sick that day
If you'd just missed your shift
If you'd rescheduled that date

I'd give it all up
If your parents had called you back home
If you'd been nestled safely in bed
Not out there on that road

I'd give it all up
If you'd just woken up late
Your whole schedule pushed back
No dark appointment with fate

I'd give it all up
If I could've just given you a call
Told you what you mean to this world
How much you matter to us all

I'd give it all up
To change even one small thing
Which, who knows, may just have changed
Everything

Digital Eulogies

A life taken
A family shattered
And yet we offer little more
Than social media chatter

An entire person
Summed up in a few heartfelt lines
The complexity of your being
The radiance of your shine

A mere footnote
For the glorious tapestry that you were
A whirling galaxy
An infinite universe

Yeah, every article
Every picture, every post:
A mere footnote,
         At the most

CORY KRUSE

Digital Eulogies II

We memorialize you in sand,

And, for a time, the tourists arrive in droves.
Sheepish and silent, they huddle in close.

Peering in, they read the words.
They offer their condolences;
They chase away the birds.

For a time, they pay their respects,
And as bad as it is, at least there's that.

But then the tide rises—
As it always does—
And your memory gets lost,
Drowned out in the flood.

A memorial of shifting sand—
How very foolish of us.

Soon, those tourists head off—
In truth, so do we—
Feeling the call toward distant shores
And other attractions down by the sea.

Digital Eulogies III

Your face lit up my feed
At least for a day or two
But then the world moved on
As it was only taught to

Highlight Reel

A timestamped album
Of your public highlights
Is all we got now
To remember you by

Highlight Reel II

A life now lived in reverse
—no forward, just back—
The Benjamin Button curse

Those You Left Behind

It's not fair
And I don't mean for me
I'm talking about your friends
Your coworkers
Your family

Those who knew you the best
Those who loved you the most
Those who felt their entire world
Answer to your gravity's pull

People like your sister Katie
Who'd only just had her baby
A beautiful, precious little boy

You'd nicknamed him Bubba; you'd prayed for him often
You'd thrilled at the prospect of buying him toys

But now that little guy
—Who you'd only once held in your arms—
Has to grow up without his auntie
Never knowing the depths of your heart

And then there's Zoie, your goofy little Pom
Who's probably still waiting
For you to come on back home

Hell, we're *all* just waiting
For you to come back home

Dream Catcher

Last night I dreamed us together;
We were shopping for food at Hy-Vee.

For some reason, we kept losing each other;
You'd wind up down the way, an aisle over,
Or always just a step or two ahead of me.

I followed after,
But you were always just out of reach.
Still, I could hear your footsteps, your laughter,
Your childlike sense of glee,

And so I chased you until I was blue in the face.
Up and down those aisles I ran,
As though someone had constructed a maze
Out of that place.

Later, inexplicably,
We were buying beers and eating chocolate,
The two of us laughing together
Now that we were finally reunited—

Before the scene abruptly changed once more,
And we were suddenly driving to your funeral,

Where you turned to me and, with tears in your eyes,
Kissed me on my forehead ...
Before whispering goodbye.

Funny, the absurdity of dreams—
And how, sometimes,
They get things just right.

Survivor's Guilt

I feel guilty for not feeling sad enough.
I feel guilty for wasting my life.
Am I a monster for these smiles I've had?
Am I broken for the tears I haven't cried?

Though ... *is* there a proper way to grieve?
Is it only in hair-pulling laments
And in glass-shattering screams?

Or should I be honoring your memory
By swallowing that lump
And committing to live this life fully?

Still, no matter what,
I know I'll feel guilty.

I feel so damn guilty.

November 10, 2020

The last time we spoke
Was just any ol' interaction.
It hardly meant anything at all.

The last time we spoke,
You got me laughin',
A pun so cheesy I couldn't help but call.

The last time we spoke,
I told you how funny you are
Without ever saying the words.

The last time we spoke,
You lit up my screen with those emojis,
Two little smirking, round-faced nerds.

The last time we spoke,
The conversation ended far too soon,
Though neither of us fully shut that door.

The last time we spoke—
Why, oh why,
Hadn't I known to say more?

Lighthouse

I didn't even know you all that well,
And now, I never will.

Hadn't learned all the things that mattered—
But, even still:

Your light *changed* me.

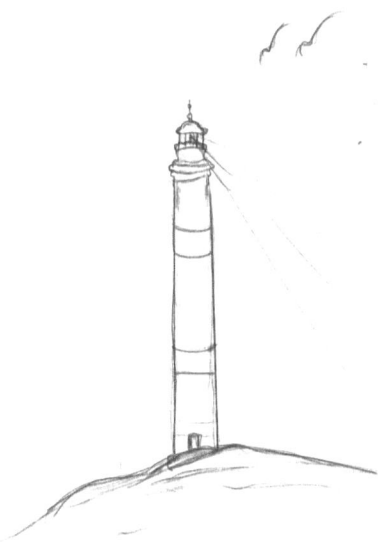

Bittersweet

You were my best race
You were my worst false start
You were the thorn in my side
You were the song in my heart

You Were / You Are

You were wicked smart
You were as classy as can be
You were pure sophistication
And yet were always laughing

You were a soul on fire
A heart a thousand miles wide
You were a mind that was always turning
And a storyteller for life

You were grace and compassion
Joy and curiosity
You were love and affection
A glimpse into eternity

You were *so much*—
And, I know now,
You still are

You still are

Inked

You had a tattoo
That read *persistence*

Maybe that's a message now
Meant for us

One Day

I'll find you in another time, another life
In fields of golden green

Perhaps then we'll be together
In a panoply of dreams

The Human Condition II

Try as we might
We can never stay the same

We're here for a moment ...
And then we're gone

The Great Beyond

If you're not scared of death,
You haven't thought about it hard enough.

Lately

Lately, I've been thinking about my death day.

Will the sun be shining on that day?
Or will it be a wedge of clouds
That carries me away?

And what will my friends have to say?
Will I be the first, or the last,
To be called away?

I know we'll all be missing each other, either way.
Man, I hope none of us are alone
When we come to that day.

CORY KRUSE

Grim Reaper

We'll all face our dying day
We'll all yearn for the days that have gone away

Gone too soon
Never enough time

Such is the curse
Of this paltry thing called life

"Keep Okoboji Blue"

A boat windshield covered in spray—
A million glittering diamonds,
So easily wiped away.

Blinders

Humans often make the mistake
Of thinking we have time.

That's ridiculous;
Time has *us*.

Metamorphosis (or, Nesting Doll)

Every moment brings about a new me,

    my past selves

        stretching off, unreachable,

    into eternity.

The Circle of Life

The thing about seasons:
They end.

All of them, in their own time,
Up and fade away.

And then ... well, then the cycle
Begins again.

Changing Seasons

It's an irrevocable truth of childhood:

Every kid has a summer when he grows bored,
When those old childish delights no longer appeal.

    The wonder fades. The shine wears off.
    The imagination wilts ... and dies.

It's like the smoldering of leaves
On a crisp September morn.

    A smoldering—which is actually a *rotting*,
    Dressed up as a spectacle of color,
    A maturation of hues,
    One we all recognize but don't acknowledge,
    At least not until it's too late.

Not until those leaves have all let go,
Until their arthritic stems have shaken loose, and relinquished their hold.

Not until they've fallen from their perch in sorrow,
In disgrace:

    A tumbling funeral procession
    That will one day
    Make fodder for our rakes.

Those leaves will be ground into pieces:
Dismembered corpses destined to become ash.

>   They'll be scattered among gutters
>   And sewage drains
>   And thick garbage sacks.

>   They'll litter lonely side streets and neglected lawns;
>   They'll flare up in burning piles—
>   One last blaze of color, before being forever gone.

Yes, they'll be raked and burned and lost upon the wind,
Swirling off to nowhere ... then summarily forgotten.

Though we'll feel their presence all the same—

>   In the crunching of our soles,
>   In the bareness of the trees,
>   In that silent wailing for color:
>   A chorus of grating branches, left sad
>   And lonely.

We'll feel the absence—the scarcity of color—
While not quite fully grasping an equal change within us,

>   A burgeoning melancholy rooted deep.

GRACE IN THE DIRT

Silent and forlorn, we'll go on our way,
Proud members of society, no longer chained

    To those old childhood follies
    Or any other such display.

(... but, in our dreams,
We won't be able to help but to wonder:

    What on earth has happened?
    Where, oh where, is all the color?)

It's an irrevocable truth of adulthood:

That same kid, though now buried deep,
Will one day look to the past ...

    And ache for that summer back.

Childhood's End

I can see it in my parents' eyes:

I'm slipping away.

The boy they raised:

Fading ...

Changing ...

Gone.

The Circus and Its Clowns

Another day of dressing up
Another day of pretend
String up a tie, paint on a smile:
Let the day begin

We all got the Sunday scaries
We all dread that 9 to 5
We're all craving something deeper:
A purpose for this life

We're all performers in a fool's play
We're all dancing on our strings
We're all crying beneath our makeup
And suffocating from these dreams

We're all laughing at a funeral
We're all weeping at the circus
We're all addicted to those things
That always wind up hurting us

Another day of dressing up
Another night of numb exhaustion
Week by week, just burning out
Forever going through the motions

Field Dressing

We get all dressed up
To go nowhere at all:

Flimsy bandages
Meant to fix bullet holes.

4:59 p.m.

Is this all that life is,
Long stretches of work
Interspersed by moments of fun?

Five days of shit,
Then two days in the sun?

Waitin' out the clock,
For these weekdays to be done?

I tell you right now,
That's not a race I want to run.

But what choice do I have?
What choice does anyone?

Sisyphus

It's a slow erosion,
The disintegration of our dreams:

We spend so much time
Rolling one stone uphill

That we don't notice the avalanche
Spilling down from the other side.

The Dregs of Splendor

What happened to the kid I used to be?
What happened to the boy who could believe in anything?

What happened to me chasing the spark?
What happened to a dreaming, love-drunk heart?

What happened to my shameless passion?
What happened to my string-free compassion?

What happened to joy and wonder?
What happened to rain and thunder?

What happened to self-love,
And knowing I am enough?

What happened?
What *happened*?

CORY KRUSE

The Art Critic

The more I look at a thing
—No matter how beautiful—
The more I notice its flaws

The longer I spend in its presence
—No matter how alluring—
The quicker I am to yawn

Why is my heart so fickle?
Why does my affection wane?

Why can't wonder last?
Why can't *anything*?

Gripers

Funny how
In the winter, we long for sunlight
But when summer comes around, that orb is just too damn hot

Funny how
We pine for spring, but we curse the season
The moment its mud mucks up our shoes

Funny how
We dream of oceans, then grow bored with the waves
As soon as we're seaside

Funny how
We long for company
Only to resent them the second they come on by

It's funny how ...
It's funny how ...

Glass Half Empty

The world used to seem so big
Now it just seems so small.

What if life is not some grand adventure
But just a slog through it all?

As We Age

I see it, right now,
The writing of our lives.

I see *who* we shall become,
I see the paths we shall tread,
I see the people we shall be.

I see the great journey away from who we *were*,
Who we *are*, into this new and inscrutable thing:

A lifting, but a plummet too,
Childlike wonder vanishing
In the face of something new.

I see the children we were, buried away.
I see a lifetime of regret, and heartbreak,
And far too many bills to pay.

I see a memorial of wrinkles and scars.

I see our damaged and lovesick hearts.

We used to chase the fireflies—
Giggling on fields of summer green.
We used to dance beneath the stars at night,
Not a care in the world if we were seen.

We used to run free with our friends.

We used to know days that would never end.

But now ... now we sit
        And we drink
        And we talk about the weather.

Now we sit
        And we drink
        And we talk about nothing at all.

Yeah, we used to chase the fireflies;
Now we only talk about the weather.

We used to chase the fireflies;
Now we pray things will get better.

Fan Service

I yearn to go back;
I have this unshakable nostalgia
For simpler days.

But here I am missing this present moment,
Which, soon enough,
Will also fade away.

CORY KRUSE

The Human Condition III

Squandered blessings
Curdle into lifelong regrets

The Hallmarks of Time

I'm petrified by an image of an older me
Rocking in an armchair
Just regretting things—

All the moments I took for granted
All the people I refused to see

—Cursing this failing flesh
And the selective nature
Of my half-gone memory

Rising Dough

You wanted to bake cookies; I remember that clearly
2:00 in the morning, and you'd never been so cheery

"Come on," you said, before racing up those stairs
Like a kid on Christmas morning, with nary a care

I followed you into the kitchen, ever so slowly
Thinking didn't you know
Now's not the time for such foolery

There're rules for this sort of thing
As adults, we shouldn't have chocolate this late
Plus, I've been counting my calories
Carefully monitoring my sugar intake

Yet you carried on, giddily grabbing a pan for that dough
Licking your fingers sweetly, dancing in the microwave's digital glow

Looking back, I know now I messed up
I should've eaten those cookies with you
I should've shared that milk cup

I should have held you close
Should've put your head on my shoulder, and your hair to my nose
The two of us just dancing together
In the warmth of that stove:

Expanding hearts
And rising dough

Lakes and Mountains

I missed your bachelor party
Logistically, it just didn't make sense

Now here I am no less tired
And rotting with regret

Higher Ed

I filled out that application for Hawaii,
But I never got around to hitting submit.

If it'd always been a dream of mine,
Then why couldn't I go through with it?

Devil's Den

I wish I would've moved Heaven and Earth
To find that jet ski

I wish I would've thrown it all away
Just to feel your arms wrapped around me

I wish I would have walked, even alone,
To that row of late-night bars

Mile after lonely mile
Just for one more chance at winning your heart

I wish I didn't have to wish
But could instead feel your breath brushing against my cheek

All these days later
And I'm still wishing that you and I
Could somehow be

CORY KRUSE

Dogs and River Walks

If I knew then what I know now
I would've done everything in my power
Not to let you down

Privilege

There's an old man down in Shantytown
With two glass marbles for his eyes.
He lifted a wave, a toothy smile,
And started tittering as I walked on by.

I strolled away, through the marketplace,
But my mind never left that old man's side.
What misfortune had led him to that alley?
What tragedies did that crooked smile hide?

That age-old question then came a-bubblin':
Why him, and why not me?
Was it some matter of choice that separated us?
Or had I merely gotten lucky?

I so often take for granted
The circumstances of my birth.
I lord around like "the chosen,"
Strutting across my inherited earth.

So often I ignore my privilege,
Spoutin' off about personal responsibility.
Believing in compassion on principle,
But refusing to get my own hands dirty.

So many times have I wasted my blessings,
 Just walking on by, and doing nothing.

I am so tired
Of doing nothing.

GRACE IN THE DIRT

Floods and Helicopters

Amazing how easy it is to take things for granted
Until you're about to lose them

Hourglass

One of my biggest fears in life:

Not having enough time
To write down all the stories
I have bouncin' around in my head.

Barely Scratching the Surface

Going to the bookstore is always bittersweet:
I absolutely love it, but I'm always reminded
Of all the books
I'll never have the time to read.

Couch Talks

I could've matched your enthusiasm
I could've showed you I cared
Instead I let you down, with yet another impassive stare

One day I'll yearn for these conversations
That seem to go nowhere at all
I'll go and pick up my cellphone
Before realizing I've nobody to call

Talking to you is the greatest blessing
Sitting beside you is a priceless gift
I wish I could just enjoy your company
Without my mind always going adrift

I wish I could get to know you before there was ever a me
I wish deep inside my eyes
Love, and interest, is all you would see

I wish, most of all, I'd never have to let you go
But time is a cruel hourglass
One whose sand is always running
So very low

I'm Sorry

For every time I missed Mother's Day
Every half-assed card on which I scribbled your name ...

For those TobyMac tickets I wasn't able to use
Knew I'd let you down; in some ways,
I'm *still* trying to make it up to you ...

For that weekend when I ruined Date Night
Asked me for a favor, yet I just took my sweet, sweet time ...

For all those twilight cruises I didn't fully enjoy
Had my pops right beside me, but my eyes were on other toys ...

For those birthday treats you brought down to the field
Went out of your way to do so, yet my embarrassment refused to yield ...

For all those jokes I just took too seriously
Insecure in my pride, always answered so furiously ...

For not having your back when it would've mattered most
A coward "too busy" to let you in close ...

For every call I didn't make
For avoiding the tough subjects, as I watched our family break ...

For every gift I took for granted
Blessing upon blessing I'd have just as soon abandoned ...

For a lifetime of countless mistakes
For waiting until now
To give forgiveness chase ...

I'm Sorry II

My "I'm too busy"
Has often meant
"You're not a priority."

For that,
I'm so, so sorry.

Prospector

Too many times
People have been too good to me
And in return
Have only received my apathy

Too many times

Too many times
I didn't know what I had
A gold mine before me
Yet I didn't bother to bring a pickaxe

Too many times

Too many times
I've picked a flower, as if I could somehow *own* its beauty
In time it always wilts to dust
And all to appease my insecurity

Too many times

Too many times
I let fear dictate my actions:
A doe-eyed animal panicked into flight

Too many times

Too many times
Have I stayed quiet when I should've spoken up
A witness on the stand whose lips are sewn shut

Too many times

Too many times
Have I lived my life as an observer:
A stagehand, not an actor
A waterboy, not a factor

Too many times

Oh, too many times

Waffler

I let every good thing slip away
And all because I can't commit to a course

Always shunted about every which way
Like a listless buoy, caught in a storm

The King of Missed Opportunities

You said, "Okay kid, this is your shot."
I'm not even sure whether I heard you or not.
I was giddy but scared, and afraid of looking weak.
Inevitably, then, I made it all about me.

I swear I tried, but in a month or two,
Just like always, my chances were through.
I let you down; I could see it in your eyes.
Still you kept me around, picking up my slack each night.

Too often, I'm too dumb to see.
But now these missed chances are weighing heavily.
I'm a fool, unwise, and maybe a tad bit lazy:
      Yeah, I'm the king,
The king of missed opportunities.

"College is the best time of your life."
Yet I spent my time broken, barely gettin' by.
"It's where you'll meet your lifelong friends."
Yet every weekend saw me packin', heading for home again.

I could've stayed in that fraternity.
I could've found help for that hurt in me.
Could've joined up with clubs and intramurals;
Instead I stayed stagnant, just feeling terrible.

Too often, I'm too dumb to see.
But now these missed chances are weighing heavily.
I'm a fool, unwise, and maybe a tad bit lazy:
      Yeah, I'm the king,
The king of missed opportunities.

You were the girl that lived down the street.
A heart of gold and a love to read.
You'd drive by in that white car of yours,
Said, "Stop on by if you ever get bored."

I loved you then, this I knew,
But I feared I'd blow it if I moved too soon.
So I let that white car drive right on by ...
And thus I watched you drive out of my life.

Too often, I'm too dumb to see.
But now these missed chances are weighing heavily.
I'm a fool, unwise, and maybe a tad bit lazy:
      Yeah, I'm the king,
The king of missed opportunities.

Tape Recorder

I'm always replaying conversations in my head
Rather than focusing on the new ones in front of me,
Instead.

Optometrist

Be careful when you blink—
Life doesn't.

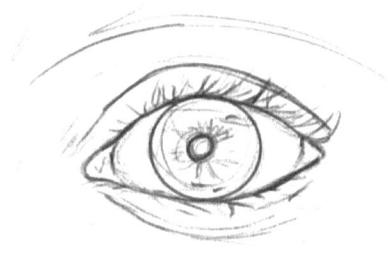

Competing Against the Clock

It's easy for us to want lost time back;
It's much harder to cherish it
While it's still here.

Backstabbing

We betray ourselves
When we waste our time.

Every second spent on worthless things:
Another jab of the knife.

Quarter-Life Crisis

I haven't done a thing—

No, not a thing
Worth doing

Reconnaissance

Every day, it feels like I'm wasting away
Squandering my life by just staying this way

Even thinking these thoughts is another mistake
Too distracted to realize I'm choosing my fate

Missing life's wonders until it's too late
Just looking ahead to some other place

Yeah, I'm always looking ahead
To some other place

A Soul in Conflict

I long for an organized world,
For peace, and order,
And routine.

But at the same instant—
I long for chaos,
For adventure,
For uncertainty.

For the great plunge into the unknown,
Away from home.

From the Nest

If I leave
Will it set me free?

Or will I only be left
Wanting?

Fickle Heart, Fickle Soul

Do I want to move on
Because it's the right thing?

Or because I'm bored
And it's simply the next thing?

Can one find their path
Without spitting on their blessings?

Or is every step forward,
In some ways, a forfeiting?

CORY KRUSE

Wanderlust

Half of me wants to leave;
The other half aches to stay.

I fear either choice may end up a regret,
Come my dying day.

For, if I don't go see the world,
Who knows what things I might miss:
    The people I might meet,
    The places I might see,
    The *me* I might get to be.

But if I do venture out, will I be abandoning
The grass I was given to grow?
    My friends,
    My hometown,
    The people I love the most?

(I think of Mom, Dad, Tyler, Nicole.
The dogs, Emery—
All of whom will have to grow up, and grow old, without me.)

How does one find true contentment, then?
Because even if I were out there in the world,
I know I'd be missing them.

But if I remain here planted, I know I'll regret
All the things I never got to do.

And yet I have to choose.
I have to choose.

"Home Is Where the Heart Is"

Home is where the heart is ...
Or so the expression goes.

Problem is,
My heart can't seem to make up its mind—

Pulled a thousand different ways
To a thousand different climes—

So, then ... do I have many homes,
Or none at all
I can actually call mine?

Escape Artist

I never arrive on a scene
Without a getaway car

An exit strategy
A sheltered heart

I never go anywhere
Without a backup plan

Loose change in the pocket
A bus ticket in hand

I never lock a door
Without holding a spare key

If there's anyone who's getting out
It's gonna be me

Horizon Chasin'

What a strange sensation it is
To be in the mountains and wanting to leave,

To be resort-laying, beachside,
And longing for a different breeze.

What a curious feeling,
To be smack-dab in the middle of paradise

And still left wondering,
What should I be doing with my life?

What a bizarre desire, always wanting to go
While, at the same time, being desperate to stay.

A tug of war of the heart,
One that's never going away.

"Only Boring People Get Bored"

The human curse, I'm quite sure,
Is boredom.

It fosters discontentment,
Greed,
And any other number of evils.

(Creativity, too, if we're
Wise enough to reach for it.)

Everything we need,
Right there in front of us
And still, we'll long for something else,
Something "better."

We'll poison ourselves with an unseen cup
While the remedy sits waiting, nestled just so
In the palms of our hands.

The Cancer of Apathy

Why is it that human beings, during times of crisis,
Can accomplish incredible feats,
And yet
We waste away during peace?

How do we keep that vigor going
At all times,
For all things?

How do we locate wonder
In the midst of feckless
Cacophony?

Horizon Chasin' II

I'm chasing something
But I don't know what

Just keep slammin' tea
From a coffee cup

Living in denial
Until the end of time

Won't stop runnin'
'Til I see the light

Thing is, if I could just slow myself down
Take a moment, and look around

I might find that that thing I've been chasing
Has already—and always—been perfectly found

Blinders II

We always assume we'll have time
Don't we

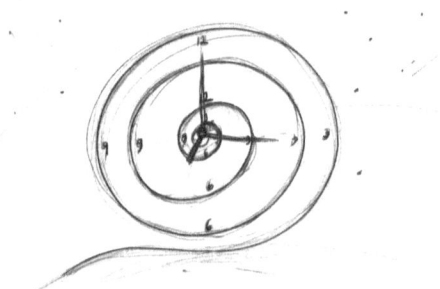

September 5, 2011 (or, Saying Goodbye to Our First Dog)

Death is so hard, even though you were only a dog.

Because, in truth, you were so much more than that:
You were a pet, a sister, a friend.

Thanks for growing up with us these past fifteen years, Cassie.
We'll love you always. Rest in peace.

Family Reunion

Death brings us together
Like no wedding ever could

"Happy Birthday!"

I find them in a box under my bed:
All are opened,
A few left unread.

Gaudy in color, cheerful in design.
A younger me ripped them open
And plundered the cash from inside.

Meaty tears plummet now as I hold them in my hand;
How could I've been so dumb?
What didn't I understand?

Because now all I got are birthday cards
To fill this you-shaped hole
Left in my heart.

Yeah, all I got now are birthday cards,
While you—you went away
With my whole damn heart.

Treasure Hidden in Plain Sight

What if the moments we wish away
Are the ones we should be most afraid to miss?

Pet Peeves

What I'd give
For another chance to be annoyed by you
The cheesy lines, all the stupid things you do
(I'd roll my eyes and probably chuckle, too)

What I'd give
For one more of our morning runs
I grumbled and complained
Until those damn things were done

What I'd give
For one of those stories you've told a million times
I'd sit and listen
And pretend not to know every line

What I'd give
For your impatient manner
All the get-up-and-go's
All the aimless chatter

What I'd give
For another poorly planned adventure
I'd tag along no matter what
Just as long as we were together

What I'd give
For just one more day
What I'd give
If I just had the chance to say:

"All those things that I thought didn't mean a thing?"
To me ... they are everything."

They are *everything*

An Obvious Reminder

Note to self:
Spend time with them
Before it's too late

The Human Condition IV

We can't choose our families;
Nor do they choose us.

You Didn't Sign Up for This

I'm certain my parents love me;
But lately, I've been wondering:
Do they *like* me?

Pecking Order

In the end, whether they mean to or not,
Every parent has their favorite child.

And all children, whether they're aware of it or not,
Know exactly where they stand.

I, for one,
Know *exactly* where I stand.

A Trip to the Zoo

I wish I didn't let you down
I wish I was who you wanted me to be

I wish I could change myself
I wish you would love me
With no uncertainty

But I can see it in your expression:
If not an indifference
Then a misperception

A bemusement
A detachment
An unsurety

The hesitation of a cook
Forced to use another's cutlery

My movements are of passing interest, sure
But when it comes down to it
There's little more than that

It's the cool regard one gives a strange creature
Sunbathing behind a pane of glass

So I shut my eyes ... turn away ...
And simply let you pass

... and you always pass

Rhetorical Questions

How many times has my laziness
Let you down?

How many times
Has my poor planning?

How many times over the years
Have I made you and the family
Regret me?

"I Don't Care; What'd You Wanna Do?"

I've been too tired
To think about your needs.
But what would it cost me, really,
To just let you take the lead?

Isn't that what you crave,
What that restless soul of yours seeks?

Or are you just looking for an honest companion,
For someone who will tag along
And delight in your company?

The Eyes Are the Windows of the Soul

I can see the years in your eyes
All the weight of days gone by

I can see the regret of what never was
An urge to start over, even if it's the end of us

I can see the anxiousness
I can see the claustrophobia
I can see the conflict, the love,
The paranoia

I can see it all; I can see it all

I Wish I Were More—For You

For the first time, I wondered if my dad was happy.

I wondered if he ever imagines different people
Sitting with him here
At the table.

If he ever yearns for better company,
For people who are funnier, smarter,
More exciting.

If he is disappointed in the direction his life has taken.
If it, in some small way, feels like he's settling;
His dreams, all but forsaken.

(And I can't ignore the fact
That at least a part of that
Is because of me.)

Does he still love my mom?
Does he burn with dreams
Left undreamed?

Is he proud of us kids?
Or are we merely strangers
Wearing faces like his?

Are his smiles fake?
Does he feel slighted, disenchanted,
Caged?

Does he regret the lifetime of choices
That he's made?
Or does he blame it all on us,
And on the trappings of fate?

The Last Supper

The silence hangs heavy between us:
A family gathered at dinner
With nothing to say.

Together, we skirt the elephant in the room—
Truth is, it's more like an entire herd:
All the topics we can't bring up;
All the scars, the silent battles, the hurts.

Remember when we used to laugh together?
When every joke didn't feel like an affront?
Remember when we didn't walk on eggshells
And the present company was more than enough?

Now—now, it's like there's a Judas sitting among us
And each of us suspects the other.
Afraid to disclose too much feeling,
Not in the midst of a traitor.

Now—now, it's like we're all so damn tired,
Trying our best to preserve the spark
Without knowing the first thing about fire.

Tongue-Tied

If only I could speak up
Then maybe I could fix this.
Maybe I'd have the power
To steer things right.

If only I could speak up
Maybe we would come together,
And none of us would have to pretend
We're not dying on the inside.

If only I could speak up ...
But, as of yet, I haven't quite been able
To find the proper words.

Tongue-Tied II

When's the last time we told each other,
"I love you,"

And meant it?

Blinders III

We think we have time
We think things will always stay the same
We think it'll go on and on
For forever and a day

We're wrong

Thief in the Night

One day I'll long for those friends who used to call
One day I'll dial my mom and won't get through at all

One day I'll crave Dad's paternal touch
A hug, a pat: never took advantage enough

One day Emery's eyes won't gleam so bright
Their curiosity, their wonder, dulled by the cruelties of life

One day Nicole's laughter won't fill up that kitchen
Don't know what we got until the sound goes missin'

One day Tyler and I will go our separate ways
Say goodbye to our antelope home, this magical place

One day ...

One day
We won't all still be together
Life will pull us apart like a poorly pasted glue

One day
I'll have a whole house to myself
And will give anything to be back here
With all of you

One day ...

CORY KRUSE

Chronometer

I got these dreams,
But I got this family:
How do I balance both
When time keeps on dwindling?

Are all these hours worth it?
Trading precious days
For some "ordained" purpose?

Or will I one day come to resent these books
And the price their creation demanded?
Surrounded by shelves of bestsellers
Just thinking about the people I abandoned?

But if there's one thing I know,
It's that throwing it all away
Would only leave me hollow.

Plus, those same loved ones always say
They always want me to be *me*:
To keep following this heart,
To never stop chasing these dreams.

So, then, how best to do so
When there's a war in this heart
And a hurricane in these bones—

Knowing that no matter who wins,
It'll be a victory tinged
With sorrow.

Overthinking III

One day I'll miss those dinners
Yes, even the awkward kind
Yet here I am still missing the moment
Trapped here deep within my own mind

Overthinking IV

now I'm overthinking about
overthinking oh god what is
wrong with me

I'm Sorry III

I'm sorry for every time I chose work over you
Asking me to swim, to go on a walk
To watch a movie, to play with the dogs

I'm sorry for every time I was distracted
When I was lost in my head
Instead of giving ya my full attention

I'm sorry for not being
Who you needed me to be, for putting myself first
And just leaving you empty

I'm sorry—but I also understand now:
Apologies don't mend ripped sails

Needles do

The Ties That Bind

Blood is a poor reason
        To stay together

So, it's time now
        We found our common ground

    Together

Hearing vs. Listening

I was so busy wondering if you were actually listening
That I forgot to listen myself.

But for no longer—
I promise you, here and now:

        I'm *listening*.

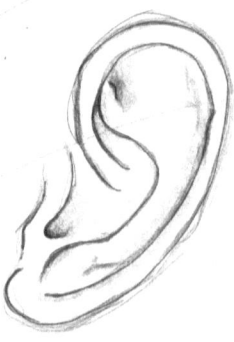

Parental Controls

What dreams led you to this moment?
What passions and fears
And heartbreak?

What obligations steered you onward?
What tough choices did you have to make?

What things unearthed your smile,
Back when that smile was new?
What hobbies injected you with life?
From which god did you take your cues?

I ask you to pull back the curtain,
To push aside the actor and show me the crew.
If there's one thing I desire the most,
It's to know the real you, under you.

Who *is* the real you?

Role Reversal

Most parents are afraid of their kids growing up without them around. Maybe we should be afraid, too, of our parents growing old without *us*.

Primary Sources

Lord,
Remind me to read the pages
Before the ink fades away.

Bubble Don't Pop

You were running around on the deck with the dog.
Plastic wand in hand, you were blowing bubbles
And chasing them until they popped.

Chortling as Abby swallowed those iridescent spheres whole,
That dumb mutt jumping and barking
As though there were no tomorrow.

I stepped outside and watched the two of you play—
Smiled as you darted up and down
And every which way.

Surrounded by an inverted waterfall—
Each bubble catching the sunlight like a dozen tiny mirrors—
Your laughter lilted higher and higher,
A giddy soundtrack for those wayward spheres.

I stood there and wished I could freeze the moment,
Could cement the three of us in time,
But I knew all those bubbles would eventually pop—
No matter how smooth the delivery, nor how gentle the flight.

I followed one with my eyes,
A refugee from that dog-'gator's ferocious jaws.
I traced it as it floated skyward, a marvel of symmetry and endurance
And simple, unremarkable luck.

Losing it in the slanting rays of sunshine, I turned to you instead.
You were squealing with delight, totally unselfconscious,
A crown of watery soap drenching your forehead.

Bubble don't pop, I thought, as I observed your glee,
Mind both on you and on that one sphere that'd broken free.

Whatever you do, whoever you decide to be,
Please just promise me:

You won't ever pop—
No, not for anything.

"Happy Birthday!" II

There was a cake
But no candles

Gifts
But no bow

Most of the chairs were empty
But you didn't let your disappointment show

I was there out of obligation
Trust me, at first, I didn't want to be

But I changed my mind the moment
That perfect smile was directed at me

I wish you had a hundred friends
I wish you never had to know pain
I wish the joy you gave others
Would more often come back your way

I wish you knew how precious you are
I wish you never once doubted our love
I wish this life would unfurl before you:
A never-ending gift from above

I wish this world was kinder
I wish you had the freedom to chase your dreams
I wish differences were celebrated
And there was an abundance for your needs

I wish I was better; I promise that I'll try
Because no matter what
In me, you got a friend for life

The Best Thing I Have

I have only this love to offer you;
I hope it's enough.

  I hope it's enough.

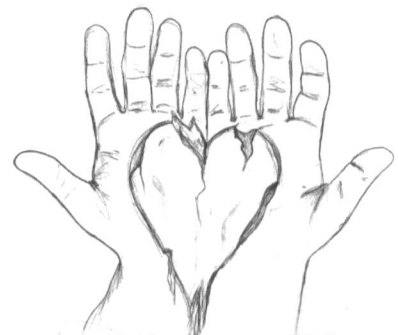

CORY KRUSE

The Human Condition V

We're all happy
Until we're not

We're all free
Except from our thoughts

We're all aching
As we play pretend

We're all lonely
Right up to the bitter end

Pathfinder

This path is a familiar one;
I can see the grooves worn by my two bare feet.

It loops around through the forest,
Taking me over and over
Past the same clump of trees.

I tread it

Because I must.
Because there's a safety in familiarity.

And because stepping left,
Or stepping right,
And heading off into what's yet unknown,
Scares the hell out of me.

This path is a familiar one;
I can see the grooves worn by my two bare feet.

CORY KRUSE

Circuit Living

We're stuck in grooves
We think will take us forward
But they only spin us

    'Round
        And around

    And
        Around

    And
        Around ...

Hesitation

Why do I do
The things that I do?

What on earth is stopping me
From going after you?

Why do I do
The things that I do?

Another path before me
And still, I know which one I'll choose.

Why do I do
The things that I do?

Why does anyone? What if there *is* no choice
For me and you?

Why do I do
The things that I do?

I wish I knew;
I wish I knew.

Progeny

We're all children
Of our worst mistakes.

We adopt their mannerisms.
We wear their smiles,
Their complexion,
Their eyes.

We sling their weight upon our backs—
And carry them for life.

Time Traveler

What is a year?
A month?
An hour?

What is forward,
When there's only back?

What is healing,
When you can't escape the past?

CORY KRUSE

Pathfinder II

I see the folly of my ways
I see the love I gave away
I see the man I used to be
I see all those who were there for me

I can see all of it—
But I can't see the path ahead

Lost in the Maze

I'm alone in a big wide world.
Hell, even on the inside:

In the depths of my heart,
In the labyrinth of my mind—

Always looking for a way out,
But just keep stumblin' forward,
Blind.

False Summits

As a child,
I dreamed of climbing that mountain.
I gazed at it from my bedroom window
Day after day after day.

You see,
I loved the glimmer of its peak,
The heft of its shoulders;
I loved the improbability of it,
The challenge it offered.

Likewise, I relished the idea
Of being able to tell others just how high
I'd managed to climb.

But you know, the funny thing is,
Once I finally got the nerve to assemble my gear,
Pack my van,
And drive to the base—

Once I was finally strong enough to lug myself skyward
And stood on top of the world,
Right there at the tip of that shimmering peak—
I didn't feel happy.

I just felt … empty.

One Day Away

I thought writing a book would save me
Turns out it only depressed me

Thought it'd fill this gaping hole inside
But it only made it deeper
And twice as wide

I thought life would suddenly get better
If I could just hold that hardcover in my hand
Thought I'd finally "make it"
Arrive grinning and free in some Promised Land

I thought my soul would be brimming, and bright,
And full
Now I just feel numb, and tired,
And oh so very old

And yet here I am—
Still putting ink to the page

Placing my hope in impassive keystrokes
And in a future that's always just
One day away

CORY KRUSE

An Escape to the Cage

Writing has always felt like
My secret thing

My hobby
My passion
My curse

It's always felt like
An ace up my sleeve

A hedged bet
A backup plan
A ticket out

Like an escape from regular life
The humdrum of that corporate-living
Weekend-chasing
Soul-sucking nine-to-five

Lately, though, it's felt more like
Delusion,

Like a hobby I've thrown up
On a pedestal

And I'm the brainwashed disciple
Devoting my life to the worship
Of some stupid, lifeless idol

Existential

"Come home," you said to me
But here I am, still chasing these dreams

And truth be told, I don't know anymore
What's the point
What's the score

Truth be told, I don't even know what I'm trying to be
Or who I am
Or who dreamed these dreams

Truth be told,
I don't know anymore

I just don't know anymore

Purpose vs. Identity

Is my only worth
Found in these books?

If I wasn't an author,
Who would I be?

If all else is stripped away,
Who am I, really?

Han Solo

In a vast world of color and noise
I am alone

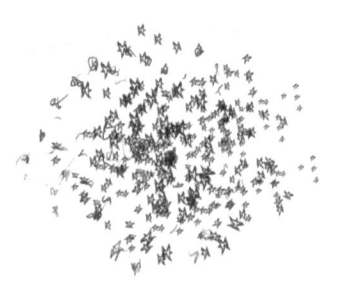

Indifference

I don't have friends
I don't have enemies
All I got
Is this world's apathy

Just Passing Through

A lot of acquaintances—
No real friends.

Smiles in passing—
Never hear from them again.

It's like I'm a man set apart,
And not for some higher gain:
An outcast, an outsider;
Ain't worth knowin' my name.

Missing Pieces

It's not that nobody gives me attention;
It's that I don't know how to *keep* their attention.

A million things to talk about,
Yet I can't think of a thing to say.

It's like I've forgotten how to properly interact,
Like I've lost sight of what it means to be "normal."

Like I have a stack of puzzle pieces—
But no box to use as a guide—

And like a few of those pieces may have gone missing
Or were perhaps just cast aside.

(Or maybe
I'm just not interesting enough
To want to talk to.)

People laughing;
I'm never in on the joke.

Yeah, mostly now,
I feel like a joke.

Circus Clown

Maybe I'm just a one-trick pony:

I can make ya like me for a night
Then lose my charm, come first light.

Or maybe I just can't relate to anyone;
Man, this life ain't much fun.

I tell you what—
I sure as hell ain't having fun.

Imposter's Syndrome

I fear I'll never live up
To the idea of me.

That, at any moment,
People might find out who I am,
Really:

A fraud.

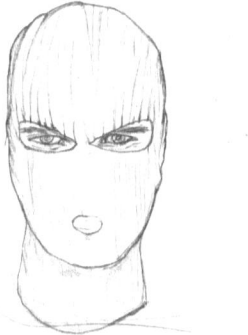

All Aboard

I'm at a train station;
I left my ticket at home.

And now all my friends are moving on without me,
And I'm left standing here at the gate,
All alone.

Masquerade

Will I ever find something real,
Something true?

Is it even possible
For someone to ever really know
The real you?

Daydream III

I want a girl I love to kiss
I want a face I'll always miss

I want a heart that beats like mine
I want a friend with whom I relish spending time

I want someone who will choose me
For me

More and more, though—
That's starting to seem unlikely

For who's going to love
Someone as broken as me

(But still ... a guy can dream)

CORY KRUSE

You Reap What You Sow

I'm alone in the worst of ways;
What else is there to say?

...

Except, maybe:
I made me this way.

Self-Imposed Exile

This whole wide world is so damn lonely;
I'm starting to think no one will ever truly know me.

Nor is anyone calling for me anymore.

But, if I'm honest,
I'm the one who slammed the doors.

If we're being honest—
I'm not even sure *where* the keys are stored.

Yeah, it's just me now—
And so many locked doors.

CORY KRUSE

The Hermit

Is there hope for a broken man like me,
So lonesome, lost, and afraid?

I've made a place of residence here;
I've sequestered myself to this cave.

The walls are dark and grimy;
The rough-hewn floor cuts up my feet.

There's a constant sound of dripping,
But never any actual water to be seen.

If I choose,
I can look out through the mouth of the cavern,
Into the glorious world beyond.

But the longer I've stayed,
The more that brightness
Has only served to burn my eyes.

And so, uncomfortable
—Always so uncomfortable—
I slink back into the darkness, away from the light.

Erosion

Wind sweeps the wasteland
      But it does not move me

Its arms kick up sand
Its teeth bite and sting

      But it does not move me

Its currents ripple and flow
Its hands beckon and pull

Its gaze roams the highlands
Soaring out toward distant valleys
Rich with amber and green

      But it does not move me

Its wings sail off over the horizon
Flattening a circuitous path in their wake
A helpful trail meant to be followed

      But it does not move me

Wind sweeps the wasteland—
Wearing me down, smoothing out the edges
Fashioning something cold
And austere and bleak

Its mouth eats away at all that was
And all that could be

      But it does not move me

The Human Condition VI

We're all broken
In our own way

"Love Yourself"

Not good enough
Seems to be my default setting
It drives my every thought
Word
And move

Not good enough
It's a restless ache inside of me
A contemptuous little whisper, always
With something to prove

Not good enough:
You're not good enough

The Miracle of the Human Body

Freedom is a falsehood.

We're not even free from our own bodies:
Hunger, shelter,
Bowel movements, sleep.

Beholden to the demands of a sack of flesh
That will always and forever
Be oh so very weak.

Performance Review

I hold disciplinary reviews with myself in the mirror.

I critique my love handles,
My flat chest, my beard.

I call the face looking back "ugly,"
"Fat," "scared."

One that's weak for its wrinkles,
Pathetic for its tears.

Well, it's those tears I take with me
As I finally manage
To crawl myself out of there.

Friendly Fire

There are days when I hate my face.

Isn't that just sad?
Being disgusted by something
So fundamental to who I am?

It's the last thing we want to show to the world,
Yet the first thing others see.
Just a simple drumskin of flesh—
Not actually the real you, or the real me.

All the same ...
I find myself ashamed
Of that gap between these teeth.
Of the bags beneath my eyes,
And the pockmarks on these cheeks.

I find myself resenting a face
That's always been wholly mine:
Traitorous thoughts for a companion
Who will be with me for life.

Self-Sabotage

I hate myself, so I poison myself
An act I'd never even *think* about doing
To somebody else

But I've found it's easier
To find the beauty in others
Than to recognize it here at home

So, I drink that poison down
Washing out every good thing
I have coming my way

Blessing by blessing:
I throw them all away

Craftsman

I chip away at myself
Little by little:
Correcting the flaws,
Smoothing out the wrinkles.

Obsessed with perfection,
Desperate for a redo.

Using a hammer
When just a paintbrush would do.

Counting Macros

"Just eat one fry."

If only you knew how my mind
Will torture me with this statement
For the rest of the night.

Counting Macros II

"Just stop eating."
I wish it were that simple.

Counting Macros III (or, I Wish I Could Stop)

"Cheat day" has, for me,
So often meant "binge day."

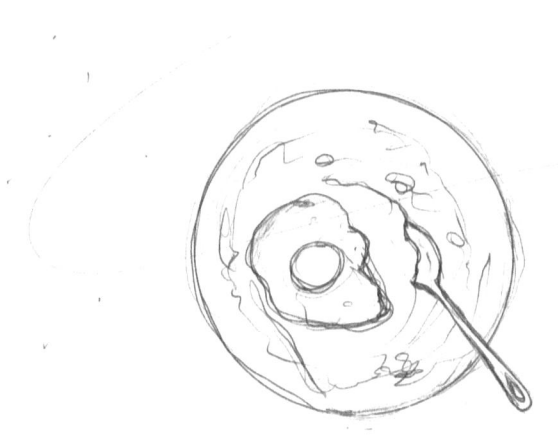

The Binge

It's all about balance,
    They say.
What they don't know
Is that I'm lashing myself
    Over and over
In an effort not to cave.

And if I do—or should I say *when* I do,
As it's always just a matter of time—
It won't just be a *cheat meal* or a *cheat day*,
    But a complete meltdown
From the inside.

CORY KRUSE

The Binge II

A dose of shame
To stave off the hurt

The Binge III

Stomach burstin'—
Ashamed
And
Miserable

But there may still be room for more

Inner cursin'—
Depressed
And
Guilty

But isn't this what cheat days are for?

Danger flirtin'—
Yes
No
Maybe

Please—oh please
No more

The Binge IV

I binge eat when I'm lonely,
Bored, sad, or tired.
I'm lonely, bored, sad,
And tired because I binge eat.

It's a vicious cycle,
One that makes me feel in control—and out of control,
All at the same time.

It's a little itch that never goes away,
No matter *how* I might fight.

It's always loitering there in the shadows,
Waiting in the dark recesses of my mind.

Though, even so ... I fight.

Dichotomy

I ain't happy
But I ain't sad
Could someone please tell me
What's up with that?

I ain't lost
But I'm far from found
Dread the thought of flight
With my feet still on the ground

I ain't okay
But I'm better than I could be
Got hope in this breast
Alongside a hole there inside of me

And on and on it goes—
That struggle there inside of me

Invisible Weight

Everyone else seems so light and whole,
While me—I got this heaviness on my soul.

Totaled

I'm starting to think I'm broken—
And maybe beyond repair.

Hurricane Season

There's always something;
There's never nothing:
Even paradise has its storms.

Black Clouds Always Trail After Sunny Days

Deep down,
I know this sunshine won't last,
That tranquility can never hold.

On the horizon:
There's always a coming storm.

CORY KRUSE

Perpetual Twilight

If there is light in death
Then there is dark in life

A hidden shadow
To every sunrise

Soured

Life is fleeting moments of pleasure
In a world gone wrong.

So. very. wrong.

Light vs. Dark

Why does darkness strike with a hammer,
While the light woos with a whisper?

Why does it seem like all the good things
Are always
Outnumbered?

No Nightlight

Remember when the darkness
Was just something that came on at night?
Now it's like a shadow
That dwells behind my eyes.

Remember when sleep
Came free and easy?
Now it's a playground for regrets,
All those various things
That haunt me.

The Pull of Night

Lie down in the darkness

    says the voice in my head

Come set down your burdens
Come rest upon my bed

      I hold tight to my lantern, with its tiny, anemic glow,
        considering, for the first time, going it alone

Come, child, just lie down in the darkness
Come surrender to the night

    I see it, then, as I lose my will to fight:

      the darkness is a bed
      and a haven
      and a noose

    Regarding that sanctuary, that void,
      I carefully set down my light ...
      But, for the moment, remain upright

Poltergeist

I haunt odd hours of the night,
Because I'm increasingly aware
I don't belong in the daylight.

Or maybe it's just that
I can't bring myself to face this life:

A fate not of my own making;
Someone else's grand design.

Or maybe I'm just scared
That the fault is actually all mine.
The choices that I've made,
Forever keeping me so very blind.

CORY KRUSE

Winter's Approach

A scattering of leaves on my soul:
Oh, I've never felt so old

Winter's Approach II

The trees are barren;
The leaves have all scattered:

I can feel them crunching
Underfoot.

The sun's gone cold;
The wind rattles these bones:

I can taste the knife
Of winter's approach.

The fires burn low;
The birds have no home—

And me?
Well, I'm losing hope.

Cold War II

I'm running scared, I'm running blind,
All the while convincing others
I'm perfectly fine.

We all got private battles.
We all got secret wars.
We're all acting put together
While keeping all of these locked doors.

We're all strangers in the end, maybe even to ourselves.
Can we ever truly know someone,
Or is isolation the fate
We've simply all been dealt?

"There's Nothing Like the Real Thing"

Manufactured emotions
Seem to be my favorite currency.

But that's because they're the only thing lately
I seem to be able to muster from me.

But hey—what can I say:
At least I'm still trying.

At least I'm still trying.

Empty Tank

I'm tired—
A bit lost and confused.

I'm tired—
Nowadays, just runnin' on fumes.

Labels

What'd you call it
When I don't enjoy *anything*
Anymore

Food
Movies
Friends
Family

Boat days
Books
Vacations
Reality

Of course, I know there's a word for it
But, truth be told, it's one I don't dare speak

As doing so would feel like
I was somehow
Making it a part of me

CORY KRUSE

Change of Scenery

Why do I want to leave?

It's not the town that's broken—

It's *me*.

Current State

Lately, I've had this notion that I might never be okay
That searching for happiness is how I'll spend my days

Lately, I'm starting to think there isn't a cure for me
That I'll be stuck living this way, in perpetuity

Lately, I'm coming to believe loneliness
Is maybe just my destiny
Or maybe it's simply something
That I once picked for me

Lately—

Overeating
Daytime dreaming
Never felt less alive

Lately—

Hating myself
And all my choices
And this very thing we call life

Lately—
Lately ...

Entomology

I rescued a beetle the other day.

It was sprawled on its back
Along the concrete.

I squinted down at it as, helpless,
It flailed its little arms, its little hands,
Its little feet,

Wagging its antennae toward the sky,
As though angry.

I wondered how it had gotten there,
Wondered what forces of life
Had carelessly tossed it aside—

One flick of fate's wrist, and now it was doing all it could
Just to survive.

Leaning forward, I carefully set it upright,
Then watched with gladness
As it scuttled off into the grass, to hide.

I walked away considering my own life,
Hoping that someone would care enough
To do the same for me.

The Thin Line Between Pity and Empathy

I wonder if you'll think of me differently
When you find out how I'm doing mentally.

Will you still care enough to check up on me,
Or will it be an awkward, halting,
Walking-on-eggshells type of thing?

If that's the case ... then, well,
I'd rather not say anything.

Mime

Wanting others to recognize my pain
Is, let's face it, such a silly game—

And I'm the one to blame.

Because I wave my arms,
Kick my legs,
And try to gesticulate,

But I can never bring myself
To actually *say*
Anything.

"I'm fine" or dumb silence—
So many little games.

Trust me, I'm well aware:
I'm the one to blame.

The Contradictions of a Wayward Heart

I'm lonely, but I'm tired
Crave peace, but got desires

I'm broken, but run from healing
Grace is free, but I keep on stealing

I'm lost, but I'm scared of being found
Longing for air, even as I let myself drown

I let myself drown

Specter

I've become a shadow
Of what I once was:

Dark and formless,
Drifting on the flood.

Wandering aimless;
Fumbling in the mud.

Broken and helpless,
No life left in this blood.

Yeah, I've become a shadow
Of what I once was.

White Flags

There are days that feel like a loss
The moment I wake up

    Like I'm starting from behind
    Like I'm drinking from an empty cup

There are battles whose outcomes
Always feel predetermined

    Like I'm mere fodder for the cannons
    Like there's no sense in tryin'

There are moments when all I can do
Is sit and wait out the clock

    Like I'm hibernating in winter
    Just waiting for spring to knock

Let me ask ya:
Will it ever knock?

CORY KRUSE

Sisyphus II

Here I am writing again
With the hope that it will save me

Try Again Tomorrow

"Tomorrow will be better."

It's a promise to myself—
Or perhaps even a prayer.

"Tomorrow will be better?"

On second thought,
Maybe it's a question.

CORY KRUSE

The Remembrance of Better Days

Oh to find joy again
In the midst of this darkest night

Oh to know peace and healing
And an end to this endless fight

Oh to feel hope
As I feel nothing at all

Oh to discover wings
That could counteract

    This

        Freefall

The Apple Doesn't Fall Far from the Tree

How can I ever be a good father
If I can't give my kids my everything?

How can I ever prove my love
When they'll sense this hole,
This *not enough*?

How can I be what they need
When there may always be this shadow
Lingering inside of me?

How can I teach them to love themselves
When I can never seem to manage to do so
Myself?

How can I ever be a good dad?
Who, I ask, will ever put up with all that?

CORY KRUSE

Malia and Edward

Your wedding night—
And here you are, comforting me.

Goddammit, I'm sorry for being so weak.

I'm Sorry IV

I'm sorry I'm not a better son
Brother
Coworker
Friend

I'm sorry for the distance you feel
The detachment
The quiet

I'm sorry for not being fun enough
For being a buzzkill
For always being tired

I'm sorry—
But please know I'm trying

I swear to you:
I'm *trying*

Fully Aware

I'm a coma patient:

Even though I'm silent and inert
And my eyes are glued shut,
I swear to you that I'm listening.

So please, *please*,
Don't stop talking.

The Music of the Lost

Silence
Is the only pure melody

Smeared Makeup

I have no more smiles
Left to give

Nonrefundable

I can't find my way
Through this darkness
I can't even feel you here

If this is "life abundant"
I want a return on my share

Waiting by the Mailbox

Send me a sign
A map
A clue

Send me a breath of wind
A dove—
Any sort of herald from you

Send me something—anything—
Just so I know
I'm not alone

Incongruity

Rainin' on a sunny day
It's rainin' on a sunny day
Oh my Lord, would you look my way
'Cause it's rainin' on a sunny day

Gotten cold in this heart of mine
Yeah, it's gotten cold in this heart of mine
No sparks, no flames, no signs of life
'Cause it's gotten cold in this heart of mine

Chained while I'm perfectly free
Yeah, I'm chained while I'm perfectly free
Fetters on my hands, my neck, and both my feet
'Cause I'm chained while I'm perfectly free

Drowning though I know how to swim
Yeah, I'm drowning though I know how to swim
A mess of foam, hair, and flailing limbs
'Cause I'm drowning though I know how to swim

Yearning for love as I keep myself lonely
Yeah, I'm yearning for love as I keep myself lonely
Push everyone away, still wishin' they'd hold me
'Cause I'm yearning for love as I keep myself lonely

Lost in the dark on this one wild ride
Yeah, I'm lost in the dark on this one wild ride
Oh my Lord, would you bring a light
'Cause I'm lost in the dark on this one wild ride

The Book of (American) Lamentations

Where are you, God,
In this pain and madness?
Where are you, God,
In this doubt and sadness?

I need you now;
Won't you come down?

Where are you, God,
Through these endless trials?
Where are you, God,
Over every sun-scorched mile?

I need you now;
Won't you come down?

Where are you, God,
During these days of fog?
Where are you, God,
When despair clouds it all?

I need you now;
Won't you come down?

Where are you, God,
In these tribulations?
Where are you, God,
Throughout this broken nation?

We need you now;
Won't you come down?

Where are you, God,
In motorcycle crashes?
Where are you, God,
With all the good ones passin'?

We need you now;
Won't you come down?

Where are you, God,
In cancer and addiction?
Where are you, God,
In corrupt politicians?

We need you now;
Won't you come down?

Where are you, God,
In this senseless violence?
Where are you, God,
In all the starving orphans?

We need you now;
Won't you come down?

Where are you, God,
In racism and evil?
Where are you, God,
In a world full of broken people?

We need you now;
Won't you come down?

Rumor Has It

Where's this mercy you speak of?
Grace sufficient, love that's enough?

Where's the bleach of redemption?
The caveat of hope, the Cross's great exemption?

Where's the key to these shackles?
The *click* of the lock, my chains' dying rattle?

Where's a yoke that's light and easy?
A shouldered weight, a rest for the weary?

Where's the touch of divine healing?
Are these prayers knocking at his gates,
Or merely coating my ceiling?

Empty Skies

What if there isn't a God up there?

Worse yet—
What if there is,
And he just doesn't care to listen?

Breaking Point

I don't wanna die
But I can't keep living this way

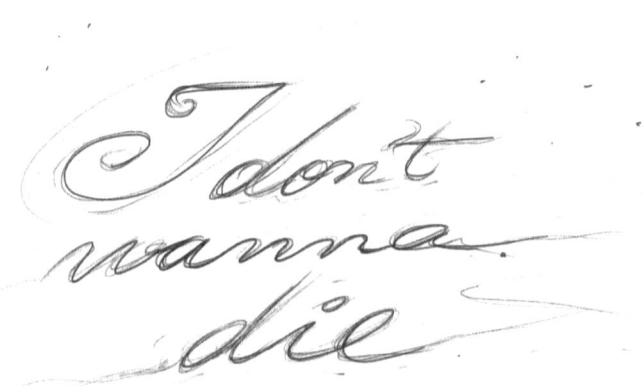

CORY KRUSE

Unfinished (or, To the One on the Edge)

You still have so many books left to read
So many places to visit, so many movies to see

You still have so many stories to write
So many people to hug, so many fires to light

You still have so many wonderful days left to live
So many meals to try, so much love to give

You still have so many things to do
So many reasons to keep being you

So please, whatever you do—
Just hold on ... and don't follow through

Man's Best Friend

I'll never forget the night
Those two dogs
Saved my life

CORY KRUSE

Eventually

I'm not okay,
But one day I might be.

Until then, I'll hold on
    Stubbornly.

Clinging tight to this life
    Here inside of me.

Doing my best to love myself
    Unconditionally.

Trusting things will get better
    Eventually,

And believing in the day
When I'll find myself free.

A Confession—Then and Now

I've hidden this truth for a while, terrified of what others may think, for how it might come to define (and alienate) me. But lately, I've also come to believe that the only way the stigma around mental health will ever end is if we address it, normalize it, confronting the topic head-on and stripping it of its power through the act of exposure. Through truth-telling. Through vulnerability. Through grace.

And so, a confession:

For the last few years, I have fought a long and arduous battle with depression, a struggle from which I'm still awaiting deliverance.

Throughout those years, I have sought help and treatment. So, too, have I attempted every homegrown remedy, including a modified diet; copious exercise, prayer, and sunlight; meditation; books on faith and self-help; and, with only marginal success, a decluttering of my life. All of it ... to no avail. This depression—this gray, inexplicable tide of melancholy—still lingers, a perpetual fog that creeps from the inside out, diluting all the brightness and beauty and buoyancy of my life.

It can permeate and cloud over entire days; at times, it can make me feel hardly alive: a mere automaton incapable of feeling emotion or harboring genuine interest in anything. Even in the happiest of circumstances it's there, always lurking at the fringes, making me feel less than whole, as if there is a missing piece, some loose wiring, sabotaging the life and purpose I was meant to lead.

It is a drowning crush of loneliness, always present, no matter how many people with whom I happen to be. It's a mind-numbing weariness with no apparent cause. It's a chasm of distance between myself and God.

It's the anguish of wasted days. Of moments experienced but not truly *shared* with my loved ones: seeing joy in their eyes and knowing it's not wholly reflected in my own. Feeling apart from them even when I'm with them. Struggling to return the love they bestow to me … and becoming all the more miserable because of it.

It's hating myself for eating a single French fry; it's bingeing on food until I'm ready to burst.

It's overthinking my every conversation for hours afterward.

It is a skepticism toward life itself, toward purpose, toward my own sense of worth. It's a nagging guilt over the untold opportunities I've bungled—all because I couldn't summon the energy to push myself into action. It's a rigorous, *incessant* cross-examination: *Is all of this my fault? Can't I just somehow will myself into being more positive? Just wake up every day and choose my attitude? What's stopping me from pushing through the fog and giving more effort?* In other words, when it comes down to it, just how culpable am I?

It's doubting I'll ever find genuine, lasting love, or that I'll be capable of keeping someone interested—much less happy—for the long haul. I mean ... who will want to put up with my silences, my overthinking, my lack of ambition? Who will stick around when things get tough, when all of life's colors seem absent or dulled? Who'll still want me?

Who will ever truly understand?

I know this depression doesn't define me, but, in some ways, it has begun to feel like something that will always be a part of who I am.

Even so, throughout this long struggle, I have been praying for God to intervene. I've been imploring him to do something, to show his power over this illness. To shine a light in the darkness. To breathe redemption into me. I've pleaded for him to hear my cries and know my pain; to simply *be with me* when nothing else will do. To grant me even a shred of his divine peace.

(Oh, how I have longed for his peace.)

However, as of yet, I haven't received it. Not more than in passing junctures and elusive intervals, which often vanish before I even realize they're there. So, even now, I'm consigned to this prison, this chasm, this season of what feels like stubborn—and, quite frankly, *cruel*—silence.

Silence, and neglect.

If God is real—and what people say about him is true—then he can heal me of this mental and spiritual agony, if he but turns my way. So why hasn't he? What's staying his hand? Is this some sort of test? A punishment? An intricate detail of his alleged plan? Is it a forging by fire? Or, is it merely my earthly cross to bear?

I don't know. But as a depressed optimist—now *there's* an oxymoron—I'm holding out hope. I'm *choosing* to do so. I'm continuing to cling to God's promises, even as my mind and heart want, at every turn, to doubt. I've seen glimpses of his presence and majesty in the past; I have my eyes peeled for the next glorious manifestation ... and the renewed hope and strength that will assuredly follow.

Despite years of waiting—and so many unanswered

prayers—I won't give up on my faith, nor on my future, despite how little I've felt lately toward either. Instead, I'm going to continue trusting that, one day, relief will come. The storm will pass. And my soul will once more know peace.

Until then, I will endure in the face of this struggle. I will endure, and I will persist.

I persist.

HOPE

Or

The Promise of a Buried Seed

It is the muck
And the darkness
From which life springs forth.

CORY KRUSE

Fallow Farming

"Barren"
Doesn't necessarily
Mean "abandoned."

Horticulture

Dormant seeds aren't dead—
They're merely slumbering.

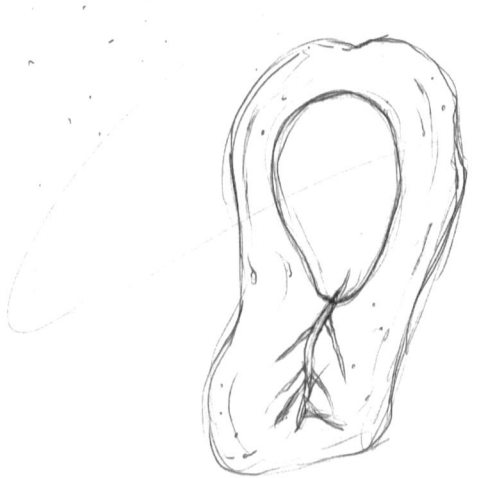

Purgatory II

Patience is a medicine.

I guzzle it
greedily.

Archeology

The season of waiting
Can erode even the highest of towers, the mightiest of walls,
The thickest of stones.

It chips away at the surface;
It grinds, smooths, chisels, drones.

Sanding away at the façade, it leaves behind something new:
A structure reshaped, reformed, repurposed;

One that's been polished down to the essentials, to its bare bones,
Roots exposed.

CORY KRUSE

The Gambler

I have found that belief is more often a choice
Than a feeling

An uncertain step forward
While you're still waiting for healing

A roll of the dice
With nothing to wager

An act of surrender
With nothing but empty coffers

Astronomy

The walls of the pit
Make for a good telescope

A focusing lens
From which to view
The whirling cosmos above

So I lie on my back, in the sludge and mire,
And force myself
To just stare up

Doubting ~~Thomas~~ Cory

My life's a lie, a contradiction
I praise your name, but without conviction

Say I believe, then doubt your love
Keep my eyes on the world, without ever looking up

From now on
I'm gonna start lookin' up

Disc Jockey

The walls of the pit
Make for a good microphone

So I'll shout into the void
Even if all I get back
Are echoes

Pleas and Echoes

Fix me, Lord
Make me new
Oh my God, I need you

Fill me up
Make me whole
God of grace, take control

Melt my heart
Revive this soul
God of love, I need a miracle

Oh God of love,
Please—*please*—
Just give me a miracle

Blessed Are the Brokenhearted

Is there redemption for me
A sinner in atrophy
Drowning in apathy
Oh Lord I plead:

Will you roll back this night
Will you grant me strength for the fight
Will you shower me with grace and peace
And light

Oh Lord
Please come quickly tonight

CORY KRUSE

Lazarus

God of glory, Lord of might:
Come and heal this pain inside.

Cover me with perfect light:
Give me strength to last the night.

So help me, Lord, if you can:
Bring me back to life again.

God of Redemption

I'm down on my knees; I've got nothing left.
So I lift up my eyes, and draw in a breath.

You're the God of redemption,
That's what they say.
Oh God of redemption,
Would you prove it today?

'Cause I have made a mess of things,
Just like I always do.
I'm drowning in the storms of life;
I swam away from you.

And I can't see through this night,
The darkness oh so deep.
Oh God of redemption,
Please remember me.

Please remember me.

CORY KRUSE

The Logic in Faith / The Faith in Logic

If God can ignite the stars
Surely he can repair
This broken heart

The Water Cycle

A drop of hope
Can dispel an ocean
Of despair

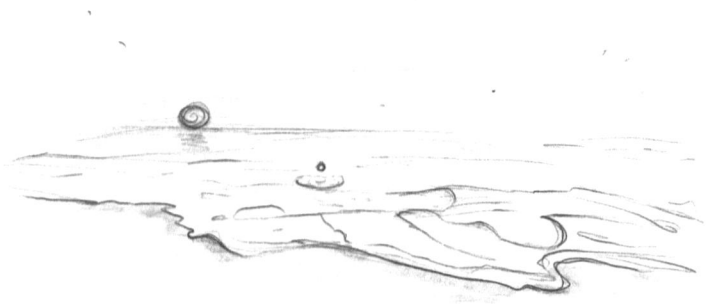

CORY KRUSE

No Time Like the Present

Let today be the day
I believe again

Let today be the day
I start again

Let today be the day
Hope comes rushing in

Let today be the day
I'm begging you, my friend

Prodigal

Bring me back to the days of hope
When fire still burned within these bones
Never worried about being alone
Because, with you, I was never on my own

Prodigal II

Show me the way back home
'Cause I'm feeling all alone
And take this pain inside
Lord, bring me back to life

And show me how it'll be
On the shores of eternity
When your face is all I need
Your love, the very air I breathe

Yeah, show me the way back home
'Cause I'm tired of wanderin' alone
And tell me that you still love me
Despite the man I chose to be

Oh, I'm begging you right now:
Come and set me free

Prodigal III

Bring me back to the days of plenty
Bring me back so I can see
That your love is all around me
And your grace is all I need

Prodigal IV

Bring me back
To the place where I knew love
Where your grace was still enough

And help me find
That I'm always on your mind
And you've been with me all this time—

And that there's still hope for this heart of mine
Redemption for the dreams that died
Healing for every tear I've cried

A joyous welcome
Once I find my way back inside

Prodigal V

Meet me at the gates
With open arms and a smiling face

With sounds of celebration
Following after in your wake

And the promise of redemption
As you usher me into that place

CORY KRUSE

The Comforter and the Comforted

One day, every tear will be wiped away.

Every tear.

And that's a promise.

The One Who Dreamed Up Spring

I got a gray soul, filled with rain
I got a black heart, drowning in pain

But you—
You can make me new

I got probing hands that yearn for more
I got wicked eyes that opened the door

But you—
You can make me new

I got a gallon of doubt for every droplet of faith
I got the credibility of a liar, with the backbone of a wraith

But you—
You can make me new

For you have a heart for new beginnings
And bringing beauty out of endings

You breathe life into the broken, the dead, the inert
You spin songs of reprise, of awakening,
Of rebirth

So I know you, Lord—
You can make me new

CORY KRUSE

At Dawn, Look to the East

Hold on, hold on:
Light will break through.
Hold on, hold on:
Rescue is coming for you.

Hold on, hold on:
This is not the end.
Hold on, hold on:
I've heard you, my friend.

Hold on, hold on:
And I promise that you will see.
There'll be a break in these clouds
And a calm to these seas.

But you gotta hold on,
And keep your eyes on that door.
Just hold on, my child,
For a little while more.

Hold on; hold on.

Coals

Hope may just be a smoldering ember, a spark.
It may just be the faintest glow in a sea of black.

But one day—surely—
It'll outshine even the sun.

CORY KRUSE

Dawn's Great Light

Soon hope will break through.
The night will fade; morning will come.
And we'll dance in the sunlight,

    Free.

Whispers and Hurricanes

When life is screaming its problems—and you feel like there's nothing left but to shout your frustration—wait, and listen for God's gentle whisper amidst all the noise:

"I see. I know. I love.

"I *move*."

The Wanderer's Prayer

I've thought about checking out at least a thousand times
But instead I'll turn to you, just one more time

Give me a reason to stay
Give me a love to light the way
The hope to carry on
And the joy of a song

Give me an answer to these prayers
Give me a sign to know you're near
The warmth of your embrace
Please don't hide your face

Oh, please don't hide your face

I've thought about giving in and letting despair take me
But I'll cling to this prayer, even as the tempest shakes me

Give me a reason to stay
Give me a love to light the way
The hope to carry on
And the joy of a song

Give me an answer to these prayers
Give me a sign to know you're near
The warmth of your embrace
Please don't hide your face

Lord, please don't hide your face

I've thought deliverance would never come ...
But now there is a tear in the clouds
There's a blossom to the hills
There's a song I didn't expect, and the sweetest of chills

There's a glorious light spilling from above
And I know at last, Lord, you have come
You have come

You gave me a reason to stay
You're the love that lights the way
The hope to carry on
And the joy in this song

You're every answer to these prayers
Crossed sea and sky to show you're near
Wrapped me tight in your embrace
Revealed the love written on your face

Yeah, there's always been love
Written on your face

Sundering Clouds

I'm bringing the rain.

There'll be an answer to all these prayers that you've prayed.
A guiding hand to help you along the way.

Yeah, I'm bringing the rain.

In these dusty fields of drought riddled with pain,
No more sorrow, no more doubt, no more shame:
A new tomorrow and a brand-new name.

Because I'm bringing the rain.

So go ahead and dance like you're not afraid,
Raise your arms and let the heavens hear you sing.
And watch with gladness as this field is remade:

Yeah, peace is seeded
And your heart's been changed.

'Cause I'm bringing the rain.

Dry-Erase

I've been pardoned
I've been found
I've been lifted, right from the ground

I've been healed
I've been set free
I've been ransomed; my heart, redeemed

Phoenix

Rise up from the darkness
Turn away from the night
Rise again into purpose
Run free into the light

Come out of the dirt
Come up from the dust
Throw away the past
Shake off your chains of rust

Rest in my grace
Hold tight to my love
Believe in your worth
And know you're enough

Because of me, child,
You've *always* been enough

The Realization that Changed Everything

I am loved, just as I am;
Whether I change or not
That truth will stand:

I am loved
Exactly as I am.

The Death Throes of a Conquered Beast

It took a while—forever, really—
But one day I finally worked up the courage
To look myself in the mirror
And declare,

"It's not your fault."

I nodded, sure now, then continued:
"You gotta forgive yourself.
You gotta free your shoulders of that weight.
You gotta let go."

My depression, meanwhile, hollered in reply,
"Liar!" and "Pathetic!" and "Wrong!"

I drowned out that voice with a flood of tears,
With trembling lips,
And with those four perfect little words:

"It's not your fault."

All That Remains

It was gone.
All of it was gone
Except this, only this:

    You.

(And it was enough.)

Thank You

Clear eyes produce
The sweetest of tears.

A liberated soul,
The most joyful of songs.

And in my wonder,
I hear you singing along.

Out to Sea (or, Downpour)

The beauty of this moment
Of right here and now
Is this rising anthem
And your love raining down

'Cause there's an ocean rising up
In this gaping heart of mine
The surge of your boundless love
Like a swelling ocean tide

I lose myself upon that surf—
I've never felt more alive

Just drinking in your goodness
And shouting toward the skies

The Orchestrator

For every tribe, every tongue
Every daughter, every son:
God has made a way

For every life torn apart
Every frail and breaking heart:
God has made a way

By his son, we are redeemed
Through his blood, he sets us free
God has made a way
God has made a way

CORY KRUSE

Audience of One

The oceans
They roar for you

And the stars
They're shining, too

It's all for you
It's all for you

The skies
They paint their hues

And the wind
Is singing, too

It's all for you
It's all for you

So I'll live this life
Just for you

Even though my days
Are so very few

They're all for you
They're all for you

A Child's Song

You are enough
You are enough
You are enough for me

You are enough
You are enough
You are enough for me

Porchlight

You were my stars at night
You were a whisper of wind in the moonlight
You were the silence after a first snowfall
You were every creek's gurgling call

You are all the beauty I've ever known
You're a porchlight shining bright
Leading me back home

A Football Metaphor

You're the team captain
Leading the way.
You're the head coach
Calling the plays.

You're the screaming fans
In the stadium seats.
You're my dad, post-game,
Saying you're so, so proud of me.

You're Friday night lights
Over a Midwest dark.
You're my beloved teammates;
You're the pride in our hearts.

You're the helmet and shoulder pads
That keep me safe.
You're the thrill of competition
And the innocence of play.

You're every championship
I've ever hoped to achieve.
You're a cause greater than myself:
Many parts, but all one body.

An Excerpt

I've seen whitecaps on western Iowa seas
I've seen sun highways on ocean peaks
I've seen weeping glaciers and stars that beam
Wandering deserts and mountains that speak

I've seen sunrises peacocking for attention
I've seen thrones of cloud in a state of suspension
I've seen acts of charity without a hint of pretension
The compassion of strangers, I can't fail to mention

I've seen so much in this life—
And yet so little
A universe in motion
But I'm stuck here in the middle

I've seen your beauty in a hundred million things;
I'm starting to recognize it, now, even in me

Axis

Without me, the world would spin on.
Without God, it won't—it can't.

CORY KRUSE

Infinite God and Intimate Friend

You know, the cool thing about God:
He's infinitely infinite and yet
Still inexplicably intimate.

The unknowable
Has made himself known.

The unfathomable
Has gifted the key to his heart.

The creator of time itself—
Has known each of our names
From the very start.

Large and Small

The God of everything
Cares about every detail
Of our lives

Cherished

Why are we running so fearfully away,
When we were all so fearfully
And wonderfully made?

Brought to life by the breath of his grace;
Molded in his image,
Crafted for his praise.

Purpose given
For each of our days;
Peace in our hearts, and hope that remains.

The Measure of Love

Life hinges on the question,
    "Is God real—and if so, does he care?

"How much?
    Enough to see my hurts, my scars?
    My longings? My fears?

"Enough to meet me where I'm at?
    Enough to love me unconditionally,
    In spite of that?

        "Enough even ... to die?"

CORY KRUSE

The Character of God

The world wants you to *do something*
Or *become someone*
To earn its love.

God loves you because he loves you—
Because he's *him*
And you're *you*.

Accept that, and set yourself free.

Foil

There's nothing greater than the love of God.

Even though I'm broken, weak,
Angry, and lost:

There's nothing greater than the love of God.

Even though I'm flawed ...
Yes, even though I'm so very flawed:

There's nothing greater than the love of God.

A liar, a traitor, a cheater,
A fraud:

Still ...
There's nothing greater than the love of God.

Cocoon

Oh to stay right here forever
In the sweetness of your embrace

To just keep basking in your love
And sending up my praise

Sanctuary

I pray this deliverance will last,
That it's the destination—
Not just some temporary reprieve.

I pray it's the end to the storm,
The dissolution of the clouds—
Not merely the eye of the hurricane.

A Conversation—Then and Now

"What's bothering you?"

"It's just ... here's the thing: When it comes to depression, there *are* no happy endings."

"What makes you say that?"

"Well ... for one, depression never truly goes away. There're no permanent victories. The doctor said I'll most likely be battling this for the rest of my life, in some form or another. Which means any win I have can only ever be temporary."

"Maybe. But that's the wrong way to look at it. Does it suck? Yeah. Is it fair? No. But every time you make it through one of those dark days, every time you overcome those impulses, that self-loathing, that crushing numbness ... every time you hold on and see yourself through to the other side, that, *right there*, is a happy ending."

"But ... it's not really an ending. There'll always be another battle. There's never any finality to it. It just goes on and on and on, like some stupid pointless cycle. No matter how good things may seem, they can always just go to shit at any moment.

"And they usually do."

"Then I'll counter with this: No matter how *bad* things may seem, they too can always turn around. And they usually do. And that's the thing: Overcoming depression isn't a destination; it's a *journey*. A battle you'll have to keep on fighting. But it's worth it, and you can *win*.

"Winning doesn't mean somehow defeating depression, either; it means *making it through*. And even if you find yourself back in that dark place, even if that cycle continues on, that doesn't make those prior victories any less significant. You made it, and that's worth celebrating. Each and every time. And it shows you that you can do it again.

"The easiest way to fail at running a marathon is thinking about all twenty-six miles at once. Focus on the one you can control—that mile immediately ahead of you. That's it. That's the secret."

"But what if I can't keep going? What if it all becomes too much?"

"Then you get help. You reach out. You lean on others. And, once more, you'll get through it. Like I said, if this is truly a cycle, then that means relief is coming. Winter melts into spring; night unspools into day. Depression's very power—its circularity—is also its weakness. It might always come back, but so, too, will it always leave. Maybe not right now, maybe not tomorrow, but eventually the despair will pass, and life will roll on: toward the good, the bright, the beautiful. And you'll come away stronger, with more clarity. With more tactics you can use. So that when the next battle *does* come, you'll be able to face that one, too. And the next ... and the next ... and the next.

"No happy endings? Nonsense. The next one's always just around the bend. So hold on to it. Believe in it. *Receive* it. And trust, as they say, that things will get better.

"Because, in time, they *will*."

GRACE IN THE DIRT

Turning the Page

I know you're the God of second chances,
Of fresh starts and new horizons.

One who's higher than these fears,
Whose love can make this shame disappear.

So guide me through every stumble and fall;
Pick me up when I've ruined it all.

And then, Lord ... well, then,
Grant me the courage
To start anew.

Note to Self

Don't be afraid:
Feel him or not, God's there.

With you.

The Inevitable Descent

The mountaintop is for awakenings;
The valley, for healing.

Into the forest one must go,
In order to start the business
Of living.

Pivot Foot

Turning around
Is just the first step.

The road stretches out;
The horizon awaits.

I check for traffic.
I haul in a breath.
I glance toward the sky ...

... and take that second step.

Road Trip

Healing isn't a straight line.

Nor is it a road trip
With a single destination.

It's a journey, an excursion,
A safari, a quest.

It's an expedition,
An odyssey, a pilgrimage, a trek.

It's a voyage into the unknown,
To a place not yet penciled on the map.

And one can never know exactly
When such a journey might wrap.

CORY KRUSE

Pathfinder III

Mystery clouds the path;
Beauty colors the edges.

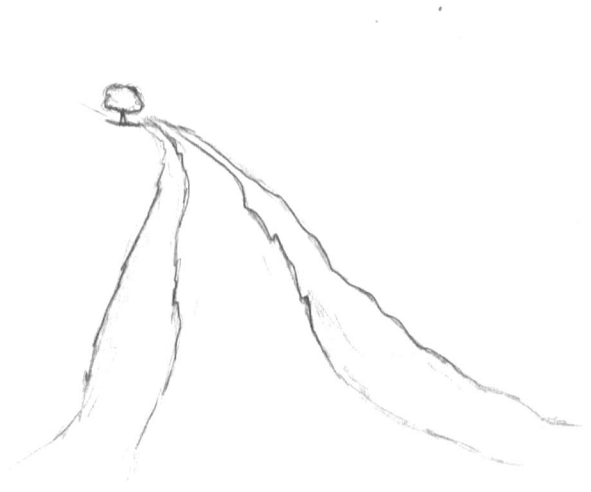

Asking the Tough Questions

Self-discovery
Comes from self-reflection

Car Wash

Never realized how grimy
The windshield had gotten.

Nor how far I'd strayed.

Pain led me in one direction;
It's time to head back the other way.

Follow the River

Given enough time,
Water will wash away any filth—

But only if it's moving.

Eustace Scrubb

Like any rough skin,
The callouses of the heart
Must be scrubbed away.

Tender Flesh

Beneath every torn-away callous
Is a patch of raw skin.

Sting though it may,
Its healing is now ready to begin.

Relay Race

I'm ready to do the hard work;
I'm ready to make myself uncomfortable.

I'm ready to claim the responsibility that's mine,
Even if
I am not entirely culpable.

I'm ready to do the hard work;
I'm prepared to do whatever it takes.

I'm gonna find the help I need
And then give redemption
My very best chase.

Mismatched

Some things you can't fix;
The pieces simply
No longer fit.

So lay 'em down.

CORY KRUSE

Altar Living

You don't have to sacrifice yourself
On the altar of love.

There's no rule that says you must be a martyr
For that which is already a lost cause.

Your relationship may have perished ...
But there'll be two deaths if you remain,
Entombed in this realm of misery and loneliness
And shame.

Misery indeed loves its company,
But here, you're its only playdate:

Your labors have gone unnoticed;
Your suffering has been in vain.

So just lay it all down,
And cast aside your chains.
Discard the compulsions that drive you;
Rise up from your chosen grave.

For, who knows,
The next chapter of your love story
May only be a few turns away.

Closure

Holding on to you
Is like holding a fistful of sand:
The harder I squeeze,
The more grains I lose.

I see it now:
It's time to let go of you.

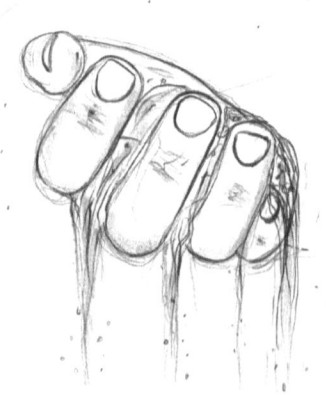

CORY KRUSE

Thank You II (or, "Whenever You're Ready")

There's a simple grace
In giving somebody else

Space

Bless Me, Father, for I Have Sinned

God, help me forgive her.
Help me to forgive *you*.

Most of all,
Help me to forgive myself.

Snow Globe

I'm sorry for all the innocent creatures I've killed
Every ant
Every spider
Every fly in a trap

I'm sorry for my blatant disregard
For forgetting that life is precious
No matter the size

Easier Said than Done

We can either fester in our regrets,
Or we can live fully—abundantly—
In spite of them.

Overflow

Every moment whispers goodbye,
But every moments teems, too,
With *life*.

Time's Indomitable Current

One thing's for sure:
Life moves fast.

We can either move against it,
Move ahead of it, or we can move *with it*,
Fully present.

Foragers

Maybe we never find our definitive purpose in life
Maybe the search itself
Is the point

Maybe that restless feeling
Keeps us from growing stagnant
Leading us from place to place
Whenever we are needed

Maybe it changes us along the way
And, in the end, maybe that alone
Is worth it

"There's No Present Like the Present"

Maybe the secret to life
Is simply being in the *now*
Wherever that happens to be

In other words, being present—
And then just doing what we can

CORY KRUSE

De-icer

When we're feeling stagnant,
It's time to stir the waters.

GRACE IN THE DIRT

Throw Back the Curtains

Fear hidden
Is
Fear renewed.

Repress something,
And you give it life.

Mountains Out of Molehills

One of the biggest hurdles of writing a book
Is getting yourself to that desk and into that chair.

Isn't the same true
For all of life?

Sisyphus III

None of my friends read my previous book.
Truth is, that hurt.

Did you write it for them? I ask myself.
All those hours; all that sacrifice; all that work?

Was it all just a ploy to earn their praise?
To put your name in the spotlight,
To have 'em turn your way?

Yes ...

Then you better just quit now.

... and no.

Let me ask again:
Did you write it for them?

Yes ... but also for me.
Mostly for me.

Then carry on, kid,
Because that, there, is everything.

Counting Macros IV

My relationship with food
Has often been tumultuous

But lately, we're finding more common ground
Between us

At last, I'm discovering that golden word
The much-preached-about
"Balance"

Man's Best Friend II

Dogs have bigger hearts than ours.

They're loyal, tender,
Earnest, and true—
And they never quite lose their appetite for play.

Oh Lord,
Help *me* to be that way.

The Apple Doesn't Fall Far from the Tree II

Hear this truth:

You don't have to be perfect
To be a good father.

Nor do you have to be whole
To be enough.

Just be their papa;
Just pour out your love.

And I promise you,
It will be enough.

Homemade Pasta

Didn't realize what I needed
Was just some time with you
I was so busy being busy
I'd forgotten this simple truth:

Life is about family
And sacrifices, too

About the small, simple pleasures
All those blessings
Hiding in plain view

So, then, in a world of distraction
I'm gonna choose *you*

Saved by a Song

You were the first girl I truly loved—
The girl of my dreams, who only ended up
Lighting this heart on fire, with lies and gasoline
Then ripping those same dreams
Clean out of me

I swore off love after that
Tired of doubling down with bad cards and a loaded deck
Blindly charging forward: no hope, no joy, no lookin' back
Just poisoning strangers with a heart gone black

But then ...
A simple love song had me turning back

I was saved by a song
I was saved by a song
When I'd given up on love
And all my hope was dead and gone

Lost and alone, scared and confused
End of my rope, with nothing left to lose
Down on my luck, with everything going wrong

Yeah, those were the moments
I was saved by a song

GRACE IN THE DIRT

You cried the day you dropped me off
Hell, I was crying too
The three of us and too many duffel bags
Packed in tight in that little dorm room

Once you left, sat scrolling through my phone
Never been so scared; never felt so alone
Until I turned on that old George Strait song
"Forever and Ever, Amen"—like a message from back home

And in that moment:
I was saved by a song

I was saved by a song
I was saved by a song
When the world grew unfamiliar
And I no longer belonged

Lost and alone, scared and confused
End of my rope, with nothing left to lose
Short on belief, with no one to rely on

Yeah, those were the moments
I was saved by a song

The day came too soon, as it always does
Standing by your graveside, kickin' at the mud
Tears on my face, all the memories of us
Looked to the sky, and couldn't help but cuss

I held on to that bitterness for far too long
Lost in regret, couldn't accept you were gone
Stayed mad at the world, at myself, at God
Until that day by the lake, with the radio turned on

And once again, as always—
I was saved by a song

I was saved by a song
I was saved by a song
When the world stole you away
And our reunion was prolonged

Lost and alone, scared and confused
End of my rope, with nothing left to lose
Numbed by grief, with my hope dead and gone

I was saved by a song
I was saved by a song
Magic in those melodies
Healing in those strums

Lost and alone, scared and confused
End of my rope, with nothing left to lose
Short on belief, with my hope dead and gone

Yeah, those were the moments
I was saved by a song

"You Wanna Know How I Got These Scars?"

If you didn't have scars, that would mean you bled out. No, those deformed, twisting little slashes of tissue mean that you survived, that you healed, no matter how ugly, at first glance, they might appear. True, they may serve as reminders of pain and unpleasantness and sorrow, but they're also undeniable signs of recovery.

Scars, then, are not marks of ugliness ...

But are declarations of *healing*.

A Broken Road

Sometimes healing
Is like the dawning of a new day
Or the blooming of spring flowers

Other times
It's like walking barefoot upon a trail of glass
With fresh shards waiting at your every step:

A shattered past
Eager to turn you back

Cracks in the Dam

Discipline comes and goes.
Sometimes it's a fortress; other times,
It's a tunnel.

Siren Songs (or, Backsliding)

Old habits call to me
Like smooth-talking friends.

They cling to me like glue;
They burn me like poison.

Just a taste, they say, ever so sweet.
You can stop whenever: just a break,
Not a defeat.

A part of me knows this is a lie.
That if I cave now, all my carefully won discipline
Will be swept aside.

And that I'll be left here disoriented
And ashamed
And resigned.
Cursing my lack of restraint,
And a failure of foresight.

CORY KRUSE

Knowing the trade-off is never worth it,
Yet having done it anyway:
Fleeting moments of pleasure
For a shame that won't dissipate.

Still ... those old habits call to me.
I turn away, but I can never silence them
Completely.

What will it hurt,
Really? those voices debate with me.
"Nothing," I answer. "... and everything."

Just One More Time (Again)

We all return to our vices,
Eventually.

(Self) Diagnosis

There goes perfection
There goes my worth

Just another lousy disappointment
Taking up space on this earth

The Definition of Grace

Darkness rose,
And the sun stopped shining,
The day you gave your life.

They killed the light of the world—
But truth be told, so did I.

So did I.

Thus I deserved your hate,
But you gave me your love.

I'd earned your wrath—
Yet it was mercy
Who showed up.

The Great Pursuer

I'm runnin', runnin' after you
Because I'm the God, the God who pursues

No matter how far, how far you might roam:
You're not alone, you're not alone

So just turn, turn back around
See my arms, my hands spread out

Ready at once to welcome you in
I call you friend, I call you friend

Chosen / Belovèd

We'll never be perfect people,
But we'll always be loved by a perfect God.

And that
Makes all the difference in the world.

Tipping the Scales

Our worth will never be determined
By another person.
Nor does it depend on our mistakes.

(Nor, even, on our triumphs.)

No, our worth has always, unshakably,
Rested on the rugged beams
Of a cross.

The Eyes of Grace

God loves us
Without blinking.

Valentine's Day

Wherever you are today—single or married, in a relationship or simply afraid of commitment—remember how much you are worth. Remember how utterly loved you are. Remember the value and preciousness each one of us holds in God's eyes, the fact that we've been given the greatest valentine of all time—the Cross.

That is a valentine that says, "I know every part of you—every hope, every dream, every failure, every defeat. I know all your fears and your regrets, the hidden pain and the buried tears. Your desire to be worth *something*, to someone. I know you inside and out ... and I see beauty, value. I love you for *you* and nothing else. And even if you don't love me in return, that will always be true. I will *always* choose to love you."

GRACE IN THE DIRT

Message in a Bottle

"Don't worry, I got this."

— God

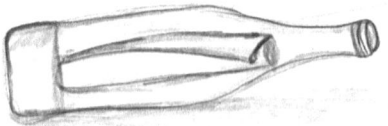

Crimson Bleach

You took my dirty hands to the well,
Where you scrubbed them
Yourself.

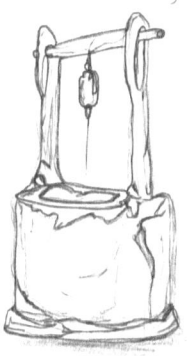

Destruction / Rebirth

Your grace, like an avalanche,
Wiped away the mountain of my sin.

Your peace, like the sweetest air,
Fills my lungs with oxygen.

You, oh Lord,
Have made me new again.

Missing the Mark

I know now
I wanna be a better man.

I long to find my way back again,
And once more be proud
Of who I am.

Oh,
I wanna be a better man.

Asking for Directions

Help me to make sense of what I don't know
Help me to keep on, and not let go

I've trusted you this far, now I need you here close
Light the path beneath my feet
And show me the way back home

Restitution

After making a big mistake,
Who are you?

Will your core character win out?
Will you endeavor to set things right?

After screwing up royally,
Will you just hide away in darkness ...
Or come blinking into the light?

The Bright Side of Failure

Failure doesn't mean defeat. Failure means a need for adjustment, for renewed dedication. Defeat only comes when we refuse to get back up, when we refuse to keep trying. Often, failure is simply the beginning of hope.

Just because we've messed up in the past doesn't mean we're spent or used up. Doesn't mean God won't still do—isn't *already* doing—great things in and through our lives. He had a plan then, and he has a plan now. So keep on hoping; keep on dreaming.

Keep on believing.

CORY KRUSE

Life's Best Teacher

Every life
Needs a few good failures

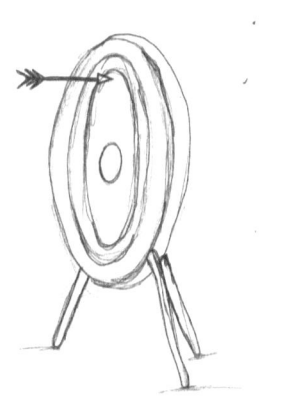

Growing Pains

Adversity is like the soreness after a workout. In the moment, it may be painful, may hurt like hell, but one day—and one day soon—it'll make us stronger, better. It may ache right now, but it's the evidence of something greater happening within us. It is the opportunity to *grow*, and if we just wait—just have faith, and never lose hope—grow we will. The pain and the problems of today will eventually fade, while the growth we experience will surely endure.

CORY KRUSE

Two Steps Forward, One Step Back

Progress is progress;
Perfection is a myth.

I've made up my mind:
I'm done with it.

"You Are What You Repeatedly Do"

Chasing perfection is a fool's errand.
Consistency, though? That's the perfect metric.

CORY KRUSE

Third-Degree Burns

Healing isn't forgetting,
Nor is it necessarily letting go.

It's a long walk through dwindling fires
With your burnt skin still aglow.

It's wounds that sting less and less,
Between unruly dreams of ice, and snow.

It's faith in sights yet unseen …
And in journey's end, with miles yet to go.

"No Loitering"

Trauma lingers ...
But grace persists.

Clarity

One day I'll look around

    And realize:

All those dark days?

    They were leading me here, to the light.

Hard Lessons (or, The Gift of Transitory Things)

There wouldn't be day
Without the darkness of night.
The sweetness of spring
Without winter's waning light.

Hard Lessons II (or, The Gift of Pain)

Even the cruelest of wildfires
Still seeds new life.

Hard Lessons III (or, The Gift of Doldrums)

Some of the deepest faith
Is found in the ruts of life.

CORY KRUSE

Hard Lessons IV (or, The Gift of the Nuisance)

Interruptions in life
Are God's way of nudging us
In a different direction

GRACE IN THE DIRT

Hard Lessons V (or, The Gift of the Struggle)

One thing I'm learning about life?
There's no permanently overcoming something.

Weight gain, fear, anger, addiction;
Failure, jealousy, shame, depression.

The light never fully beats back the dark—
Not forever, anyway.

Nor does good eradicate evil;
It's an ongoing battle.

But that means the reverse is also true:
That there's no permanently overcoming
All the bright and beautiful things, either.

Strength will rise; hope will endure.
The key is we can't grow complacent.
We must choose, each morning, to breathe in—
And then face it.

The battle goes on ...
But so do me and you.

So do me and you.

Hard Lessons VI (or, The Gift of Undulating Waves)

Feeling God's presence is, I'm learning, like being stranded out at sea upon a little rickety boat, one tossed and turned by the ocean's endless indomitable churning. Sometimes, the waves surge up—veritable monsters eager to swallow us whole—in a great wall of water and spray and foam, one that obscures even a hint of land from view. While, at other intervals, we ride the sea's mighty crests, no less shaken, but now with a clear view of the coastline ... and the unyielding lighthouse planted there. Mountains and valleys: but the shore remains the same. Whether we can see it or not, it's always there, beckoning.

Hard Lessons VII (or, The Gift of Divine Perspective)

God's timing is impeccable.

The problem is we're too zoomed in,
Scrambling to view the tapestry of his plan
From our one tiny square.

So often, then, we hunt for meaning
Without knowing the full picture;

Baffled, we squint through the wrong end of the microscope,
And wonder why on earth
Things can't be clearer.

Hard Lessons VIII (or, The Gift of Hidden Treasure)

There's still so much beauty in this world,
If you just know where to look.

Hard Lessons IX (or, The Gift of Chaos)

Chaos is life's frequent companion,
Its primordial shadow.

It drapes over every wandering path;
It shrouds every crooked turn.

But at the edges: beauty,
And the promise of boundless wonders
Still to be discovered.

CORY KRUSE

Hard Lessons X (or, The Gift of a Shattered Compass)

The best thing about a fresh start?
A blank page.

The worst thing about a fresh start?
That same blank page.

Lord, give me the courage to scribble a mark,
And the wisdom to know
What form it should take.

March 2014 (or, With Graduation's Approach)

It's both exhilarating and terrifying
To think I can do literally anything I want with my life,
And that these decisions are even now upon me.

Scribe

One day, somebody somewhere
May record our story.

What kind of tale
Do we want it to be?

Singularity

You're gonna change the world;
The very fact of your existence says so.

There will never be another person like you;
There'll never be someone who thinks,
Speaks,
Or acts
Exactly as you do.

Nor will there ever be another soul like your own;
Every breath you take, another pathway thrown.

Yeah, you're gonna change the world, all right.
The only question, then, is what sort of impact
Will you choose to make?

Called

What kind of life will I lead?
What sort of man will I be?

I've seen a million streaming lights;
I've heard a thousand closing doors.

I've felt this ache, here, deep inside of me:
An unshakable longing
To chase after *more*.

"What Do You Want to Be When You Grow Up?"

I don't know exactly what I want to do with my life, but I know how I want it to look: a picture of passion and hope, purpose and joy.

A picture ... of love.

CORY KRUSE

"No Hands!"

Sometimes we hold on so tight,
We miss the thrill of the ride.

Tunnel Vision / Kaleidoscope

If we never take time to pause, and lift our gazes,
We may miss the wonders
Spinning all around us.

Morass

Water that isn't flowing
Stagnates

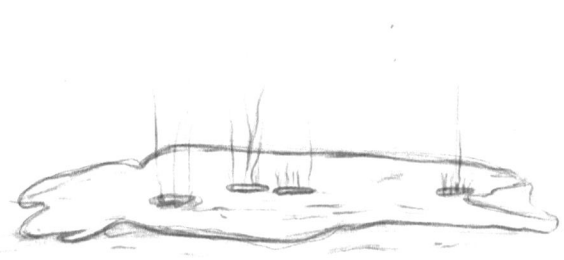

House Hunters

We so often limit ourselves,
Residing in cages of our own design.

We pad the walls for safety;
We straighten the furniture
To the pass the time.

Meanwhile, a world in color spins on outside,
Beckoning from beyond that unlocked door.

If only we could get ourselves to crawl through it,
We'd find a life of splendor—and much to explore.

CORY KRUSE

Celestial Hearts (or, The Voyagers Who Lost Their Way)

An entire universe
Resides within us

Yet we hardly ever
Leave the Solar System

Checkin' Boxes

If only we prayed
As though we genuinely believed
God was listening.

The Dreamer

God has dreams for our lives so far beyond anything we can possibly hope or imagine. The amazing thing with God, though: With him, they're not just dreams—but *plans*.

"You Can Be Anything You Wanna Be"

Why do we put God in a box?
Why do we put ourselves?

Why do we limit our lives to ordinary,
When there's greatness waiting
Right there on the shelves?

Why do we stop trying
When we were made for so much more
Than to settle?

Why do we notice all the obstacles
Instead of tallying
All of the miracles?

Because life is *still*
So full of miracles.

Note to Self II (or, The Gift of the Everyday)

The little things of today, when stripped away tomorrow,
Will seem like the greatest blessings in the world.

Life's a gift—cherish it.

The Orchestrator

God works miracles
In the mundane.

CORY KRUSE

The Ballad of "Ordinary" Lives

Most often, the great story of our lives
Unfolds within the minutiae of the everyday.

So cling to each moment as if it's a treasure,
One that might up
And slip away.

Note to Self III

Don't wait for your life to begin
Don't wait for your life to begin
Don't wait for your life to begin

Ripples

The ripples we think will never travel far
Can end up as entire waves
Splashing against distant shores

Ripples II

Believe in the power of ordinary choices
And the miracles that can come
From simple acts of love

Believe that your work here matters
That you can still do great things
No matter how often you've messed up

Believe that failure isn't disqualification
But simply *preparation*
A refinement for the battles—
And the glory—still ahead

Believe that your life is significant
That there's meaning to that beating heart
And purpose for your every breath

In the end
Just ... believe

CORY KRUSE

A Prayer of Carpe Diem

Lord, help me to see life as a gift instead of an obligation. To cherish the little things and make every day count. Help me to never go through the motions, to never take a single second for granted, and to never miss the value in any moment or in any person. Simply put, help me to truly love—to truly *live*.

For that's what life is all about.

GRACE IN THE DIRT

Every Moment Matters

If we believe in the will and plans of God,
Then what in this life can truly be a coincidence?

A Prayer for Overthinking

One of my biggest fears in life is that I'll take it for granted. That I'll miss the point, go through the motions. I am terrified by the notion I'm failing to make the most of the opportunities I've been given, painfully aware of how easily things can change and be lost forever. Conversely, I've found I'm actually missing the point by struggling so fiercely *not* to miss it. I am trying so hard to cherish life that—sometimes, ironically enough—it keeps me from doing exactly that: truly living.

So God, tonight, as always, help me to see life as the priceless gift it is. To know the value of every moment, of all the mundane and trivial things that will mean so much in the long run. Help me, then, to quit going through the motions, but also, just as importantly, to quash my overthinking and to live authentically, with gratitude and love.

Help me to let go ... and just *be*.

Walk by Faith

Let the fear fall away.
Trust, and have faith.

Kaleidoscopic Arrays of a Life on Fire

I wanna view my life like a kaleidoscope
Soak in every color, every image, every hope
I wanna find the faith I knew as a child
The imagination, the belief, the carefree smile

So, I'm gonna live like I'm on borrowed time
Bask in every moment, shove my fears aside
I'm gonna find a way to make this feeling last
A hold on the future, a curtain to the past

Yeah, I'm gonna keep these eyes on the present
And I'm gonna start livin'

I'm gonna start livin'

Life Is Infectious

If there's one thing I'm sure of,
It's that there is still so much good
Left in this world.

Special Moments

Me and Mom,
Howling along to "Werewolves of London"
After every Hunan Palace, "I'm-so-stuffed" lunch outing ...

Me and Dad,
Cackling along to nightly reruns of *Seinfeld*;
For months on end, quotin' George and Kramer to ourselves ...

Me and Tyler,
Singing happy birthday in a foreign tongue;
A perfect day of scuba, a celebration in the sun ...

Me and Nicole,
Watching that little punk making fun of our dad;
How she stormed right over, said, "That's enough of that!" ...

Me and Emery,
Singing worship tunes in the car,
Or every Chuck E. Cheese adventure, or playing laser tag in the dark ...

Me and Cassie,
Chasing each other around the yard,
Our micro-adventures leavin' me breathless, giggling so damn hard ...

CORY KRUSE

Me and Abby,
Paddling through those early morning laps;
Like two old teammates, the pair of us smiling beneath our respective caps ...

Me and Peyton,
Sprinting toward each other on that gravel running trail—
The explosion of warmth in my chest, the joyful dance-waggle of her tail ...

So special moments ...
        Too many to tell.

Four Score and Seven Years Ago

The Setting: The Lincoln Memorial, early summer (the humidity, at 9:00 a.m., already cranked up to ten), with busloads of school children scampering up and down those majestic marble steps.

The Protagonist: Me, a first-year teacher, chaperoning two dozen of those squirrelly, bright-eyed youths with a handful of parents and other more-seasoned educators, all of us standing back just then and letting the students roam. In time, we'll gather them together and sermonize about Abraham Lincoln and "The Gettysburg Address"; about Martin Luther King, Jr., the "I Have a Dream" speech, and the entire March on Washington itself. But, for now, we allow the students to explore and to feel the magnitude, the *history*, for themselves; to experience the enormity of this place, the living current of its memories, sown into the marble of each and every step.

The Plot: As the students wander about, I find myself drifting forward, up and over the smooth ivory of those stairs, past the row of fluted columns fashioned in the Greek revival style, and into the monument proper: a sprawling central hall whose glowing Memorial ceiling soars up toward the heavens, the effect on observers a dizzying combination of contraction and vertigo. I feel, at once, both important and very, very small.

My eyes find the monument's namesake statue—because how could they not? How could they ever fail to notice something so grandiose, so *large*?—but then they stray onward, over the clogs of sweating tourists and gibbering park rangers, past a line of yet more towering columns, and into the quiet south chamber. Upon its central wall is an inscription of Lincoln's "Gettysburg Address," arranged in a neat rectangle adorned with two stout pilasters, engraved wreaths, and a pair of stoic eagles standing watch over the room.

The elegant ornamentation leaves little question as to the chamber's chief attraction, though the expansive three-paneled *Emancipation* mural directly above the address vies for its own share of the attention, its trilogy of scenes serving as an allegorical companion piece to the late president's speech. My eyes trace the middle panel—the Angel of Truth, with her raised arms and gigantic golden wings, is in the process of liberating a group of slaves—before drifting to the address itself: to its huge, stately block letters, the majestic decorations around its base ... and to a quiet pair nestled beneath the words, the two of them looking totally rapt, their necks craned upward.

I pace closer, keeping my eyes on the carved lettering, not entirely sure why I'm drawn forward. Through the row of columns and nearly level with the pair now, I risk glancing their way. It is a father and a daughter, him outfitted in a patchy, short-sleeve button-up, a ballcap, and a pair of cargo shorts; her in her best child's athleisure, complete with running shorts, a headband, and a pair of well-worn tennis shoes. They're standing hip-to-hip, him crouching a little, one arm wrapped about her shoulder while the other is extended up and out, pointing toward the wall. It's then I realize he's reading to her, slow and steady, tracing the speech with his finger, careful not to lose her along the way.

I can see, too, that she's doing her best to keep up. No faux enthusiasm nor stubborn pre-teen apathy here; no, the girl appears genuinely engaged, enthralled even, as she follows along with her father's voice. At intervals, I hear her shyly pose questions to him, simple things regarding areas that don't make sense, or about oddities in the speech's old-timey language that bug her. There's the occasional "What does that word mean, Daddy?" and the innocent nose-crinkle inquiry of "Who's that?" as well as the ever-astute (and child favorite) "Why?" Even from where I stand, I can make out the sense of wonder unfolding across this young girl's face, all the way from her lips to her cheeks to her eyes.

No matter how many interruptions or curious asides—in fact, he seems to welcome them—the father never detracts from his task nor derails his purpose. He carries on, ever composed, treating this makeshift lesson as any professor worth their salt would treat their signature lecture: as though this moment, and *this* student's learning, is the only thing that matters; as though every word spoken, therefore, is significant; and as though the two of them have all the time in the world.

Watching them, I nod to myself with a soft, silent smile. And then, leaving them to it—father and daughter nestled in their own private kingdom of curiosity and companionship—I turn ... and I walk away.

The Moral: I've never forgotten that sight, as that is the type of father I aim to be: earnest, patient, devoted, and loving. Never too busy to revel in a single moment; to drop everything and just *teach*. Never letting my daughter forget that, to me, she will always, *always*, be the most important thing.

A Prayer for My Family and Friends (or, As 2020 Ends)

Lord, as I look back on this turbulent year, I want to first take a moment to pause ... and to thank you for the blessings of family, of friendship, and of continued health. The problems of this world have, at times, felt bigger than ever, but I'm reminded that *you* are bigger still. No matter how chaotic life may seem, you remain firmly in control. Even more amazingly, you remain *close*: both infinite God and intimate friend.

So, I ask you, Lord, please continue to draw near; please continue wrapping your loving arms around my family and friends and shielding them with your divine protection. But don't *just* keep them safe; let them also find happiness and peace, purpose and healing. Let them know grace in this life—and let *me* be the vessel from which it flows.

In your holy name, I pray. Amen.

CORY KRUSE

Check In on Your Friends

The happiest people are often
Those most ravaged by despair.

So no matter how inconvenient,
How awkward or touchy
Or sad:

Just be there.

To My Friends

If you ever need encouragement,
Help, or an alibi.

Or maybe even
Just an ear to listen:

I'm here.

Don't hesitate, don't doubt,
Don't fear:

Just call.

CORY KRUSE

Edward and Malia

Your wedding night—
And there you were, comforting me.

Lord, how'd I get so *lucky*?

April 10, 2021

One of the things they never tell you about when you're growing up is the joy you'll get from watching your best friend fall in love. The giddy excitement; the sense of pride. I've now gotten to experience that firsthand, have gotten to watch Brady—this big, bearded, hopeless romantic—grow into an incredible boyfriend, fiancé, and husband.

And that's what love does: It transforms us. It energizes and empowers and inspires us. It brightens our path; it reveals our purpose. It changes the world. And I know Brady and Toni's love is going to do exactly that: make this world a better, brighter place.

Today was perfect; I love you two.

Coefficients

Some constants in this world: God is good, and is never changing; life is short, and demands savoring; love is real, and is worth choosing.

It's worth choosing.

The Trade-Off of Lowered Walls

Love may break your heart
But it also makes that same heart
Worth having in the first place

CORY KRUSE

Either / Or II

One day I'll find the one for me
She'll be sweet and strong
And intelligent and funny

One day I'll find the one for me
When that day comes, I pray to God
That I'm ready

One day I'll find the one for me
Until then, I'll work on being
The best man that I can be:

Someone who's gentle and strong
And compassionate and sweet

(Someone, in other words,
She'll actually want to meet)

One day ...
I *know* I'll find the one for me

Separation Anxiety

I had a girl break my heart;
After her, a couple more.

From then on, always watching the door,
Just waitin' for the moment
They'll head for distant shores.

Fear is stronger than love.
Fear is stronger than love.
Fear is stronger than love.
"You're not enough, you're not enough."

So I kept my soul hidden;
My heart, under lock and key.
Sure they would up and change their minds,
And once more, like always, just abandon me.

Fear is stronger than love.
Fear is stronger than love.
Fear is stronger than love.
"You're not enough, you're not enough."

But then ... then I met you:
Full of sunlight and beauty
And compassion and truth.

An angel who saved me—
Who stayed, when she didn't have to.
Someone who loves me completely:
Inside and out, and through and through.

And it made me new.

Perfect love casts out all fear.
Perfect love casts out all fear.
Perfect love casts out all fear.
"I am here, I am here."

You told me, "You no longer have to be afraid.
I'll be your lantern when the skies go gray.
Your anchor, when life's storms batter you
Up and down, and every which way.

"Your sure thing today,
Tomorrow, and all other days.
Because I promise you my love won't fade away.
I'm telling you, I'm here to stay."

Perfect love casts out all fear.
Perfect love casts out all fear.
Perfect love casts out all fear.
"I am here, I am here."

You and I are far from perfect,
But the love we have sure is worth it.
In its wake, every fear shall melt away,
For, like you, I'm gonna stay.

I'm gonna stay.

Perfect love casts out all fear.
Perfect love casts out all fear.
Perfect love casts out all fear.
"I am here, I am here."

Utopia

Can you imagine a world free of shame?

How different things might be
    If grace
Were the running heartbeat
    Of society?

CORY KRUSE

Measuring Out Grace

When did petty squabbling and snarky replies
trump Christian charity?
"Love thy neighbor"—unless they differ politically.

What happened to being the hands and feet?
Did our thirst for comfort and power
steal away our empathy?

Why are we hunting for slivers,
when, in our own eyes,
we all still have these beams?

How do we call ourselves Christians
when political pride has become our creed?

In the world and of the world—
don't worry, I'm also talking about me.

Lord, revive our hearts,
And let our grace, once more, be free.

United We Stand, Divided We Fall

Nowadays, we're all so divided;
Can we ever fix it?

Will we have the strength to come together,
Or have we forgotten how to build bridges?

Me? I still believe
In what we all could be,

If only we opened up our eyes
And allowed ourselves
To truly *see*.

CORY KRUSE

The Great Commission

Love isn't complicated,
Nor should it ever be.

Actually, it's rather simple:

    Serving.

It's unconditionally caring for others
As God does—

    No *ifs*, *ands*, or *buts*—

Just loving with hearts on fire,

    No matter what.

Doppelgänger

If we're made in the image of God,
And God is love,

Then we're designed for just that: loving—
Passionately, extravagantly.

Unconditionally.

We Are Water

We are water.
We are rain.

We are tiny droplets against a steel-gray sky.
Falling/drifting/beating,
Twirling through the night.

Will we roll out to sea, together, with the rest,
Or end up mere smudges
Drying against the glass?

Eyes Forward

A simple, but powerful, truth:
Every morning is a new beginning.

So let it be.

CORY KRUSE

An August Reflection

A new school year is ahead. My heart's heavy,
But my expectations are high.
Let's do something great, create something beautiful.

Let's make it *count*.

New Perspective

Endings are guaranteed in life.
But, by that same token,
So are new beginnings—so are fresh starts.

Oh,
What a beautiful truth to behold.

CORY KRUSE

The Gift of Waking

We woke up this morning:

What more of an opportunity
Could we possibly need?

The Human Condition VII

We fly like birds;
We fiddle like bees.

We drape like stars;
We flutter like leaves.

Death is a mountain;
But life is a sea.

Yes, death is a mountain;
    But life is a sea.

God's an Artist

It's cool to think there's an entire lifetime of sunsets I haven't seen yet—and that each one of them is of a different shape, variety, and hue.

The Nature of Existence

Life is so fleeting,
But it is so, so sweet.

Old Age

You used to sculpt your body.
Now it's time to sculpt your heart,
Your soul,
Your mind.

The day you stop working on yourself
Is the day you will surely die.

Narcolepsy

Don't fall asleep
Without first closing your eyes.

Don't close your eyes
Without telling the world
"Goodbye."

Goodbye.

CORY KRUSE

The Heaven Chronicles (or, The Great Adventure)

I came to the edge of the world ...
And I dared to look over.

The Heaven Chronicles II (or, Pilgrim's Progress)

We're on the greatest adventure of all—a journey of friendship and love, discovery and growth. A journey filled with heartbreak and loss and unimaginable regret. With failure. But it's also one laden with lasting and profound joy, as well as definitive purpose and incalculable worth.

Along this path, through every valley and over every hill, we are not alone. We have a Companion to guide us every step of the way, toward the approaching horizon and what awaits us there. A place where every moment is infinitely better than the one previous, every sight and sound eclipsing those that came before. A realm abundant with surprises—and surprises of the sweetest variety: pleasant, meaningful, shared.

Breathtaking.

Never-ending.

The Heaven Chronicles III (or, Death's Defeat)

What can death do to a life fully lived? It can take *nothing* away.

What can death do to true love? It *pales* in comparison.

What can death do to the promise of heaven? It is utterly crushed beneath the weight of glory and eternal happiness that are coming. Beneath the assurance of every tear being wiped away, of the innumerable reunions that will be ours—all of which will leave our hearts positively bursting with joy.

So hold onto hope and light in this dark world. We *will* be with our loved ones again; their lives *did* matter. One day all of this will make perfect sense, and, because of a cross—because of the man named Jesus who gave his life there—death will be proven to be nothing.

No, death is defeated ... and love has forever won.

The Heaven Chronicles IV (or, Heaven's Hindsight)

One day in heaven we'll just sit and marvel at the beauty of God's intricate, perfect plan for our lives, one we're finally able to comprehend. The heartache and pain; the terrible rejections and unfathomable loss; watching our loved ones die—it will all finally make sense to us.

So never lose faith; never give up hope.

More is *always* going on than you know.

CORY KRUSE

The Heaven Chronicles V (or, Shower Thoughts)

Do you think we'll get FOMO in heaven?

A trillion, trillion things to do,
To taste,
To hear,
To see ...

But I know for each one I'll want you there,
Experiencing that fresh iteration of paradise
Right alongside me.

But what if your idea of paradise
Manifests differently? What if what I dream of
Is not, in the end, what you need?

(What if this is purely the *human* way
Of thinking about things?)

So much wonder;
So much possible impossibility.
How will we ever be satisfied when we can't,
All at once, do everything?

(Maybe, when we get there,
We'll find out we actually can
And we won't have to miss a thing.)

FOMO in heaven? What a ridiculous idea
From someone who clearly doesn't understand.
I'll tell ya what, though,
That someone can't *wait* for it all to begin.

The Heaven Chronicles VI
(or, All Dogs Go to Heaven)

I wonder what dogs dream of.

Probably fenceless lands ...
Rolling pastures ...
Endless fields of green—
And running free.

(Come to think of it, so do we.)

I hope one day in heaven
My dogs still recognize me.
I hope they climb up into my lap
And the four of us can finally speak

(Between a shower of slobbery kisses,
Belly scratches, and bacon-y treats).

I hope I can run those verdant fields with them
And never find myself growing weak.
I hope our story continues on—bright eyes, tails wagging—
Right into eternity.

CORY KRUSE

The Heaven Chronicles VII (or, 'Round the Campfire)

I'm convinced heaven
Is a warm summer night somewhere,
With a good fire
And good friends.

The Heaven Chronicles VIII
(or, Beyond Our Wildest Dreams)

The God of the bluest blues
And the greenest greens—

The one who breathed fire into the stars
And taught the oceans to sing—

The God who dreamed up sunsets and puppies
And music and ice cream—

That's the one who's preparing a place,
Handcrafting an eternal home
Just for you and me.

Oh, what a *sight* it will be ...

CORY KRUSE

The Heaven Chronicles IX (or, Flight Attendant)

Carry me over the mountains
Carry me to the sea
Carry me to that far green country
Where, at last, I will be free

The Heaven Chronicles X
(or, Arrival)

I've come home over the mountains
Through rain and stormy sea
I've come home over the mountains
Where at last my Jesus
        Welcomes me

Exeunt

The horizon gets us all, eventually.

...

Thank God for the moon.
Thank God for the stars.

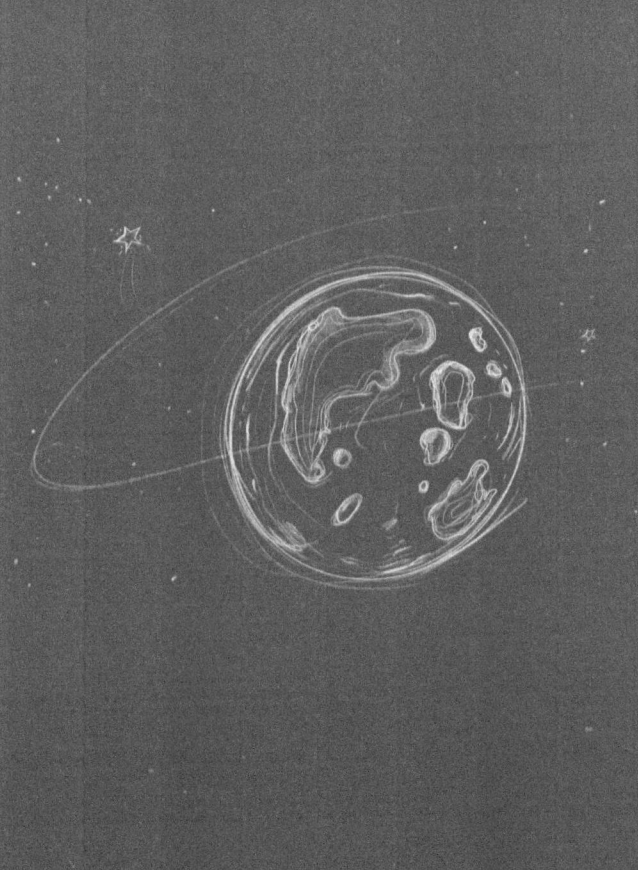

You gave me grace in the dirt.
I'd dirtied my hands, questioned my worth.

Still you showed me love of a precious kind;
Pulled me in close, whispered, "You'll always be mine."

And now I have a peace beyond my grasp,
The promise of healing: eyes forward, not back.

Yeah, I've discovered grace in the dirt,
Learned your presence dwells even in the darkest of earth,
And that there's hope to be had even when I feel nothing at all:
Strength for my weakness; forgiveness when I fall.

Once, I thought brokenness was all I'd ever know,
But I watched in amazement
As you drew near … then did the impossible.

So thank you, God, for grace in the dirt—
For joy in the sorrow, and for love that is sure.

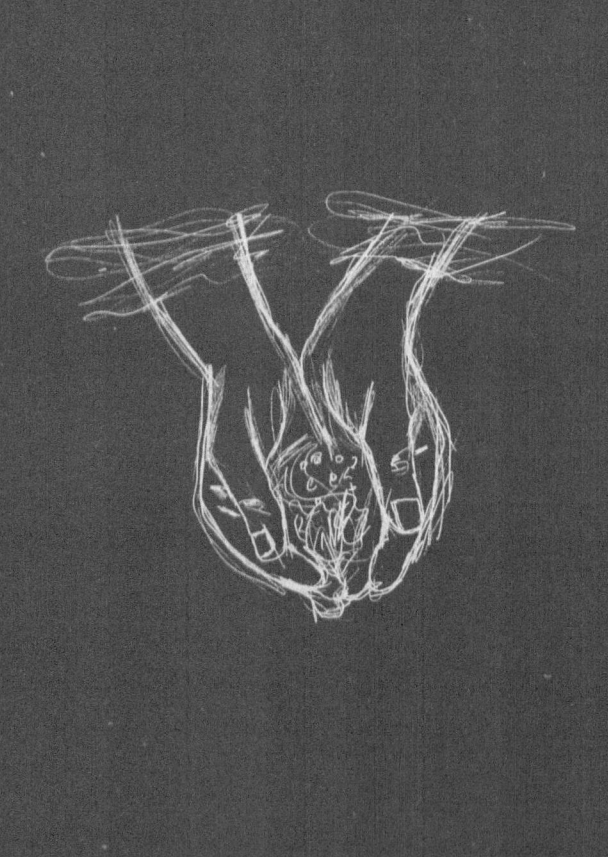

ACKNOWLEDGMENTS

Or

The Sowers and the One Who Reaped

Man, I hate writing these things.

Okay, not really. If anything, the Acknowledgments is the section to which I most relish devoting time, as it allows me the chance to reflect on the journey of a book and on all of the kindhearted, talented, and just plain *wonderful* people I have in my life. The rub? The ever-present likelihood that I'll inadvertently leave somebody out, causing no small measure of awkwardness, hard feelings, or—when encountering said snubbed individuals—prolonged moments, on my part, of foot-in-the-mouth. Compounding the dilemma is the sheer magnitude of people I need to thank, from all those who've believed in me since grade school to the community of supporters who came out in droves to champion my first book.

The solution? Ensure that, in the coming pages, I'm exceedingly thorough.

Which means all of this may get a bit wordy. (Sorry.)

First, thanks once more (and always) to my family, without whom I am nothing. Dad, you are my rock; Mom, you are my spark. Emery, you are laser tag, hide-'n-seek, and countless other reminders of life's simple pleasures. Nicole, you are gentle inquiries and constant encouragement; Tyler, you're the best friend I've ever had. In terms of my authorial career, each of you has contributed time, energy, and financial resources; even more crucially, perhaps, you've also never once wavered in your belief of this dream. Every casual conversation; every text, selfie, and Snap; every post share and act of guerrilla marketing; every time you paused to tell me you're proud: Each moment, no matter how small or seemingly trivial, lives imprinted upon my heart—an ever-growing tapestry of your love.

The members of my extended family (the Bauerlys, Bodes, Doyles, Freeds, Kruses, and Starostkas) are a source of nourishment, shelter, spiritual guidance, friendship, and— lookin' at you, Aunt Vick and Aunt T—giddy laughter. Few things warm my heart quite like our family gatherings, nor have the ability to cheer my soul like our collective tomfoolery. I can't wait 'til we're all together again—when I'll inevitably beat the lot of you in Spoons.

Any writer knows one of the first things to be sacrificed to the demands of a project is, subconsciously or otherwise, your social life. Luckily, I have an incredible network of friends who keep me sane and refreshed (and who rarely take "no" for an answer). I'm blessed to share this life—and so many riotous memories—with the following cohorts: The P's Pizza Loungers, The Football Sunday Gamblers, The Abel Carousers, and The Boys' Weekend Revelers. Additionally, I can't neglect to mention The Hawaiian Adventurers, The Omaha Imbibers, and all the colorful characters who make up the hive of miscreants and reprobates known as The Cruise Rascals. There are a lot of adjectives I could use to describe you all, but I think I'll just stick with two: patently ridiculous and utterly delightful.

Nick Wankum continues to prove best friends don't necessarily need to live in the same city, and that some bonds truly are built for life. In his seminal treatise on the craft,

Stephen King contends that every author possesses an "ideal reader," a person for whom that author writes, and whom he or she visualizes when imagining an outside party reading the completed work. Nick remains that for me—an ideal reader for whom I delight in crafting stories and characters and all manner of mythos and plot twists. His indefatigable support has borne me through countless seasons of famine and drought; his enthusiasm for the process, his detailed feedback, and his many nerd-driven (read: glorious) digressions have a way of pulling me back from despair. His friendship is, need it be said, a gift.

On the production side of things, I need to recognize (with what will amount to far too paltry a summation) the extraordinary Anamaria Stefan, who orchestrated every aspect of *Grace in the Dirt*'s design with such precision, ingenuity, and flair. From the magnificent cover on which my name is fortunate enough to reside to the seamless layout, typesetting, and illustrations that charm the inside, her work is a masterclass in artistic prowess. One of the best decisions I ever made was selecting her as my graphic designer—both for this book and for the previous. Her professionalism is unrivaled; her creativity nothing short of inspired.

On a similar note, my words wouldn't be nearly what they are without the patient, meticulous perusal of the manuscript by Parisa Zolfaghari. Leveraging a prodigious eye for language and detail, she helped transform my guttural scribbling into a collection of writing that sings. Every author is only as good as his or her editor; I'm grateful to have worked with someone as capable, passionate, and lyrically minded as Parisa.

Finally, Matt McKenzie was my stellar video designer who put together trailers for both of my books. His fantastic work helped jumpstart my marketing efforts ... and helped me believe, even for a short while, that my stories had come to visual life.

The aforementioned Tyler Kruse has been more than just a friend or a brother; he's also one hell of a manager (there, Tyler, I said it—and put it in ink, no less. Hopefully, this'll finally get ya off my back). In all seriousness, Tyler has been an invaluable asset to my PR and strategy team, working tirelessly to get the word out, secure venues, procure the necessary supplies, and help coordinate the host of other logistical details that accompany any book's release. I would never claim to be an expert on the industry, but if there's one thing I am sure of, it's that every author needs to find themselves a manager who's willing to partake in a last-minute, wild goose chase of a scavenger hunt all across town, scouring for boxes of missing product and pestering hapless delivery drivers and warehouse workers along the way. The thought of Tyler rummaging through that storage facility's debris field of packages—sweat pouring off him like the aftermath of some particularly violent rainstorm—always makes me chuckle ... and reminds me anew of just how good I have it.

Dr. Terrance Spahl trusted me to shepherd his own book from draft to publication; I learned so many valuable lessons during the process as well as enjoyed numerous scintillating conversations. Jennifer Grego of Sioux City's Sir Cuts is the best haircare professional around (you can't change my mind on that) and she is, in a word, electric. My coworkers at

Sterling make it a tremendous company for which to work, one built on passion, innovation, and, even in a corporate setting, *humanity*. Especially of note are the dedicated leadership staff and my teammates on the Sales Ops side of things—in particular, my boss, Jim Sobaski, whose brilliant analytical mind is matched only by his infectious sense of humor and his deeply compassionate heart.

As well as my favorite fellow gossip, Allie Oakley is a terrific location scout, bookmark visionary, and a bona fide aesthetic guru (I'm quite certain her love language is flannel). On top of all that, she's also a talented fashion designer and entrepreneur, one who's served as my wardrobe consultant on more occasions than I can count (and let me tell ya: She rarely minces her words). One of the best surprises these past few years has been getting to know Allie. I'm grateful for all the advice she's given, all the shenanigans we've shared ("Date?!"), and all the memories still to come. Kyle, you better hold on to this one.

While not directly pertaining to this specific book, I feel the need to call out all those who made the release of my first novel, *A Dream of Darkness*, a harvest beyond reckoning. One book always naturally flows into the next, and so this collection wouldn't exist without all those who stood beside me on that first go-round. Tom Betz bought the *first* copy of my work; even more notably, he continues to be a mentor and an inspiration—one who possesses the greatest heart for people I've ever known (as well as, perhaps, the largest memory bank of movie quotes). Kari Nelson shared her graphic design expertise (and utter kindness) while crafting the perfect promotional material for both this book and the last. Kati Brewer documented *ADoD*'s release with her wonderful photographs. And, along with always believing in my potential, Christian Bork allowed me to borrow Heelan's striking wood lectern for my first-ever live reading.

Janet Flanagan, meanwhile, spared some much-needed marketing space in the beloved *Crusader Connection* as well as taught me priceless lessons on the art of copywriting. Likewise, Jay Wright was—and remains—a "street-level" ambassador for my work, generously lending out airtime on his superb *Knights of Old* podcast (well worth your time if you haven't yet tuned in). He's also an avid lover of history, literature, intriguing sports stories, and all things mentoring. I was once a wide-eyed rascal whom he took under his wing; I'm a much better man today because of it.

The audiobook producer for *A Dream of Darkness*, Boyd Barrett, is not only a man of singular creative talent but also one of faith, compassion, humor, sincerity, and professional insight. Working with him was a godsend; throughout the process, he regularly wowed me with his producing and acting abilities as well as with his workhorse-like mentality and keen understanding of the nature of storytelling. I'm blessed to have gotten to work with Boyd; I'm fortunate now to also consider him a friend.

The cast for the audiobook—pulled together by Boyd, who also stars in the production—features an exceptional pool of performing talent. Each of the actors brought such enthusiasm, skill, and meticulous depth to their interpretations. I was astonished and humbled—and may have teared up *juuust* a little—as I listened to them bring characters of mine to life. Specifically, I'm indebted to the phenomenal Holly Adams (Ellen Breeve and Mary Fern); Bonnie Bogovich (Julie Temult, Betsy Til, and other various voices); Jaden Carmichael (Kel Pollor); Justin Fife (Thomas Calvin and Riley Ford); Madison Garrison (Natalie Willow and other various voices); Sarah Golding (Sara Ash and other various voices); Johnny Haynes (Jacob Willow); Robin Haynes (Christopher Willow); Eddie Kronfli (Codiah Longford); Karim Kronfli (Skylar Higgins); Dayn Leonardson (our remarkable composer, who crafted the audiobook's haunting musical themes with such passion and ingenuity); Pete Lutz (Peter Ash and other various voices); Agnes McCuen (Heather Ash); Owen McCuen (Brade Higgins and other various voices); Cordell Spears (Walter Reins); Riley Spears (Frederick Reins and Vernon Rose); and Sam Young (William Breeve). I am eternally grateful to each of you.

In a similar vein, I am thankful for Megan Swanson and H. R. Hutzel (author of the tremendous *BethEl* series), both of whom lent networking connections, industry insight, and simple yet essential kindness along the journey.

Brady Van Dusen was a vital errand boy (consider this payback for that recurring "water boy" joke lol), booth manager, event staff, and panicking-writer therapist—in other words, like any best friend, he's a jack of all trades who's willing to do whatever it takes, no matter how menial the task, to make a friend's dreams come true. His wife, Toni, served as my de facto social media strategist (choosing the right caption is so damn hard!) and continues to be a luminous presence in my life.

The members of "The Crazies" book club (Ellen Dirks, Laurie Dougherty, Lindy Fitzsimmons, Michele McDevitt, Erin and Teresa McElroy, and Rene Mohrhauser, among others) welcomed me with such grace and gusto—and no shortage of inappropriate (read: hilarious) tangents and asides.

Digital artist Morgan Wright reimagined my book cover and illustrations, transforming them into haunting animations that are striking *and* cool. Lindsay Hindman (SiouxlandFamilies.com) reached out and kindly reviewed an early draft of *A Dream of Darkness*; it's been a pleasure collaborating with her in the years since. Other members of the media to whom I owe a great deal include Jacob Heller, John Holmes, and Larry Wentz of KMEG 14; Earl Horlyk and Bruce Miller of the *Sioux City Journal*; the always wonderful Beth Fennel and Bruce Odson from the *Dakota Dunes/North Sioux City Times*; Stacie Anderson of *Siouxland Magazine*; Vinit Bagdai of the "Magic through Your Eyes" Bookstagram blog; and the gracious team of reviewers at *Kirkus Reviews* and *The BookLife Prize*.

In my previous Acknowledgments, I included a list of the dozens of educators who played a role in my development as a writer and as an individual; unfortunately, I failed to mention Kris Vondrak, who was—and is—such a bright light for her students, one who always leaves an indelible mark.

Finally, Christina Odom and Pat Sitzman were prayer warriors in the face of near-catastrophe (relatively speaking), who made my inaugural book signing a celebration like no other. Their giddy enthusiasm; their words of affirmation; their no-holds-barred love and sense of pride—all of it still summons the biggest of smiles. The Bible suggests that, throughout human history, angels have come down and secretly dwelt among us; if that's the case, then I'd argue these two are most definitely a pair.

A hearty round of thanks to all those who took the time to read A Dream of Darkness and share their thoughts, promoted the book via their social channels and by word of mouth, left honest reviews at their favorite retailers, or—for those less ... let's say, *literarily inclined*—supported in other ways, such as by purchasing a book for "decorative purposes" or by simply spreading the word. (Here is the place where my apprehension inevitably begins bubbling up, as I'll never be able to remember everyone. But I promise I'll do my best to list off as many people as I can. If, on the off chance, I *do* happen to miss you, feel free to send me a strongly worded—albeit polite—message decrying my forgetfulness and the utter ingratitude I've shown toward your contribution to the cause. At which point I'll respond with a contrite, carefully worded apology loaded with the appropriate emojis as well as the promise of reparations in the form of a complimentary beverage at your earliest convenience. Beer or liquor: Pick your poison. Limit one per customer.)

Members of the Kruisers (we're still workshopping the name) include the following friends and torchbearers: Claire and Dylan Adams; the Ahlers family (Anna, Jeff, Lori, and Sam [where're my *Pokémon* cards, you nerd?!]); Jimi Alan; Michael Alcaraz; Katy Anderson, favorite intern (don't tell Lauren); Jaden and Jeff Arends; Joey Awtry, the future film adaptation's producer and star; Chris and Jenni Barber; John Barber; Lisa Barton; Abby Bauerla; Molly Bauerly; the Beck family (James, Jami, Mr. Pickles, Sharon, and, of course, the vivacious Tito); Jeanna Becker; the Bengford family (Andrea, Breanne, Clayton, and Tony); Eldon Bensen; Carli Berger; the Bergmann family (Brock, Jayde, Paul, and Stacey); Linda Bernard; Brian and Wanda Berndt; Karena Beth; Giacomo Bettelli; the previously mentioned Tom Betz, who, after nearly every chapter, would shoot me a text laden with exclamation points; Dawn Bland; Heide Blatchford; Adam Bobier; Justin Bode; the ever-talented Blake Bogenrief, who was the reason I began compiling this collection to begin with; all the fine folks at Book People in Sioux City; the Bork family (Brayden, Chad, Jenna, Jill, and Kolby); Mike Bousquet; Jody Branson; Rhonda Brockamp-Bridges; Lauren Brobst; Libby Brower; Kaitlyn Brown; Melonie and Tyler Brown; Briley and Nick Buckley; Abby Burns; Jordan Brus (aka Bonecrusher); Jon Buck; Carter Buckmeier; Angel Cancino; Jim Christiansen; the Clay family (Andrew, Brad, Elizabeth, and Jennifer); JoAnn and Meghan Clemens; Denise and Jeff Clements; Keri Clifford (seen any school buses lately?); Charlotte Clovis; Chase (go drink some water, you wimp), Heather, and Jill Collins; Cassidy Condon; Katie Cooke ("Hi, Katie!"); Father Jerome Cosgrove, whose heart is always open for those in need: the epitome, if there ever was one, of being the hands and feet; the Cougill family (Brennan, Brooklyn, and Gina [aka Mama G]); Justin Coury; Adrian and Corinne Cox, the latter of whom has been a rare type of friend ever since that day she first strolled into the Wankums' basement and subsequently took the Heelan community by storm; Ignacio Cruchaga von Tramnitz (weón); Charlie and Nicole Curran; Tammy Davey; Alex De La O;

Ty Dennison; Alicia and Emily Derby; Katie Dougherty (aka Brotha, ask Dough, aka Heelan's resident conspiracy theorist for long-irrelevant student body presidential elections); Judy Doyle; Tami Doyle; Bryan Dowd, who is an unlikely cross-country supporter and friend, but one I cherish all the more because of it; and all the employees at Drilling Pharmacy.

(*Pause for breath*)

Lauren Eckert; Ashley and Jacob Elser; Ryan Fee, who's one of my favorite people on Earth ... and also one of the biggest idiots I know; Dave and Sue Ferris, both of whom are the embodiment of kindness and Christian charity; Mary Fischer; the Fitzsimmons family (Annie, Jack, Joey, John, Jimmy [don't forget to sharpen those teeth!], Lindy, Mary Kate, and Pete ["Preter!"]; John Flanery; Andres Flores; Kristian and Stephanie Freed; Jeanie Forker; Andy Foster; Kylee Full; Chase Funk; Greg Funk; Kayla and Linda Garvin; Dr. Lauren Gatti; Katelyn Gebel; Alan and Alex Gerdes; Mary Goebel; Chance Grady; Laura Grebasch; Taryn Ham; the Hanno family (Grace, John, Mary, and Madeline); Tim and Talen Hawkins; the Heaton family (Amy, Bailey, Jason, Keegan, and Simon); the *other* Heaton family (Kasey, Kathy, Kevin, and Kyle); Julie Helkenn; Katie Heller; Jayne Hettinger; the Higman family (Ava, Jerad, and Peggy); Joe and Michaela Hindman; the Hohenstein family (Branden, Jeanie, Kevin, Kyle, and Melissa); Kyle Hooks, my second big brother; Kaylee Hughes ("Normies!"); the Hupke family (Kelsey, Ruby, and Violet); Ani Hyde; Tyler Jacobs, wonderful poet and long-distance friend; Megan Jensen; Mary (Halligan) John; Casey Johnson; Camry Jones; Sheri Jones; Cale Kaiser; the

Karrer family (Brenna, Katy, Kramer, Nick, and Will); Grant Kathol; the Keizer family (Brooklyn, Shane, and Shawnie); the Kerian family (Cooper, David, Jeff, Liz, Steve, and Tina); Kyle Kinney; Lauren Kipp, favorite intern (don't tell Katy); Shane Kleier; Meg Kofmehl; Matt Koley; Dan Kriese; Rashmi Krishna ("It's Thursday!"); Bailey Nicole Krogman; Dustin Kruse (you still owe me that $444,000,000); Joe and Marlene Kruse; the Kuehl family (Carter, Kane, and Mandi); Mary Kuhlmann; Reid Lamoureux; Brittany Laubenthal (aka Blaub); Jaymi Leif, favorite bartender; Gerard Lairisa Llena; Cameron Lee; the late Jennifer Lenzini, purveyor of joy and light and beauty; Jordan Lester; Izzy Linden; Ryan Livingston; Lane Longval; and Daniel Luesebrink (aka Dirty Dan).

(*Coffee break*)

Kayleigh Jo; Sandy and Steve MacDonald; Faustin and Makayla Mahlke; Alexander Mallory (aka The Senator, aka Creature), whose thirst for life—and all of its many wonders—has proven catching, helping me to see the world with fresh eyes; Michael Malloy, who will remain family (and my running back) for life; Trevor Mandernach; Noah Marasco-Ayau; Carter Matousek; the Mattison family (Baylee, Landon [aka the Calamity of the Seas ... as well as my oldest friend], Mike, Morgan, Raejean, and Taylor); Zach Maxey, the king of stupid comments, enduring friendship, and the best cross-country surprise; Brett McCabe; the McCabe family (Beth, Kelsey, Rachel, Sam, and Tim), who put up with me (and my Husker affiliations) far more than any reasonable person should; and Zach McCabe (aka Treebeard), who deserves his own entry here, as he's always been there for me: a former roommate and an eternal best friend—even if I *did* have to force my way into his life.

(*Stand up and stretch*)

Anna McCarthy; Aaron McCoy; Sherry McCoy; Judy McGuire; Alyssa McKnight; fellow author Jacquolyn McMurray; the McNabb family (Brad, Julie, and Will); Shane Meendering; Jessica Meinen; Becky and Bruce Meyer; Devan Meyer (aka Goofy, who, through the years, has shared in so many great adventures); Kelley Meyer; Andy Meza; Sam Mohrhauser; Teo Molifua; Austin Moore; the Moore family (Brad, Jean, Katie, Megan, Rachel, and Ryan); Carlynn Moretz; Katie Mueller; Mindy Mullen; the Murphy family (Cindy, Katie, Lucas, Max, and Pat); Dan Nelson ("Nelly!"); Peter Newhouse; Mark Nickles; Ben Novotny; Katie Oberle; Sarah and Scott Oligmueller; Drew Olsen; Laura Olson; Maddie and Will O'Malley; Chief Bill Pappas; Jenny Pattee; Saška Pavlović (aka Sashy, my favorite new friend from the Windy City); Julie Perreault; Amanda Peters; the Petersen family (Amy, Anne, and Mark); Shelby Petersen (*there*, you're finally in the book—better actually read this one now); Kaitlyn and Lauren Peterson (favorite fellow *GoT*, *LOTR*, *Star Wars*, and *Binge Mode* nerds); Zack Peterson; the Petty family (Jack, Jenny, Luke, and Mark); Joe Pham; Kristen Phillips; Mike Pithan; Jake Placzek (you dirty dog); Jaicee Post (next time I see ya, beef stew's on me); Dustin Pratt; the Pratt family (Beth, Christian, Jason, and Sydney); Benjamin Preston; Beth Pruchniak; Brian Radebaugh; Jon Raitt; Sr. Colane Recker; Miranda Rector; Bryce and Kaitlyn Reynolds; Brenna Rehan; Tom Rice; Brett Rickord; Carlos G. Rios; the Rizk family

(Bill, Katie, Michael, Nicole, and Pam); Sean Roberts (aka the Sam to my Frodo); Yourna Rose; Brooke Rosener; Tracy Routh; Temple Rucker; Alex and Kristi Robertson; and Nate and Sarah Ruehle.

(*Don't worry, we're nearing the end*)

The Saunders family (Brenda, Levi, and Todd—some of the best, most genuine people around ... who also know how to make one hell of a corndog); Nick Sawin, my favorite doctor in training and former defensive end, who still doesn't know how to guard against a sweep; Kendra Schamber; Eric and Megan Schettler; Amanda Schmidt; Kelsey Schmidt (aka Fargo's Queen of Shorts); the Schorg family (Michele, Paige, Terry, and Wesley); Philip Schulenberg; Nathan Schulz; Tanner Schumacher; Steph Schumann; Lindsay Schwabe; Mindy Schweitzer, who's conferred invaluable wisdom through the years regarding marketing and editing; Garrett Seamans and family; Liz Sherrill; Carly Shideler, acting buddy; Tim Singharath; Larry Sitzman; Joe Sitzmann of P's Pizza; Yvette Sitzmann; Matt Skaggs; Jake and Katie Skibinski; Zach Skibinski; Nathan Skidmore; the Sloniker family (Barbara, Jason, Maria, and Michael); Haley Solonynka; the Spears family (Bob, Chris, Connor, and Tucker); the Spenner family (Cindy, Donn, and Mindy); the Stanley family (Craig, Jane, Joey, and Katelyn); Betsy Stannard (aka Satch, DB, and my first college friend); Natalie and Zach Starostka, the former of who regularly shares my book with her students; the Steffen family (Jerry, Katelyn, Loree, Mitch, and Natalie, as well as that speed-reader of an aunt whose name I never quite caught); Erin and Kyle Stevens, who made the several-hour trek to my first book signing (even if they are a couple of dirty narcs, I'm grateful for their friendship); Kris Stoddard; Justin Stragz; Laurie and Marley Strand-Nicolaisen; Willis Strawn; Breanna Streeter; Anthony Sunclades (aka Bernarnold), who, poor tastes in sci-fi fantasy films aside, is one of my favorite people with whom to discuss movies, TV shows, and all other forms of miscellanea; and the Svec family (Austin, Lisa, Noah, Riley, and Roger).

(*Now entering: The Final Stretch*)

Jenna Nicole Tanderup, who has to be one of the most grace-filled yet straight-up *bothersome* readers out there; Andrew Taylor; Sydney Thelen; Katie Thomas; Dr. Sarah Thomas, who taught me to think deeply, to question with empathy, to serve compassionately, and to work for justice, always; Brent and Kristin Thorn; Brooklyn Tolliver; Kenzie Tommins; Amy and Eddie Tritsch; Lisa and John Tritz; Jim and Toni Tschann; Rae Tucker; Andy and Morgan Umthun; Ed and Toni VanCleave; Sydnee Van Der Maaten; Jestin Van Maanen; Jim and Kathy Verschoor; Nick Voichahoske (aka Eric Church, Ol' One-Eyed, the other Kruse brother, and "Little Chow!"); Ryan Wadzinski; the Walsh family (Katelyn, Kyle, Lori, and Pat); the Wankum family (Ben, Chris, Jaime, and Michael), who took me in as one of their own; Taylor Warntjes; Reid Welch; Alex and April Welding; Alex and Serena Whitesell; the Wiest family (Chris, Jake, and Joy); the Williams family (Jeff, Scotty, and Shannon ["YOU!"]); Jill and Walker Woods; Ed and Tracy Wriedt ("Banana!"); Christy Wright; Thomas Young; Melonie Zublis-Brown (feelin' up to some training?); and, last but not least, the Zunino Gomez family (Catalina, Constanza, Jose Pablo, and Josefina), some of my favorite traveling companions, with whom I shared one of the best trips of my life—I hope all of our paths cross again one day soon.

If the protracted list above should tell you anything, it's that I'm supremely blessed when it comes to the friends and family I have in my life, a fact I never wish to take for granted. There are few better sources of grace in the dirt than each of you; I will never lose sight of that.

Finally, thanks most of all to the Great Sower, who harvests beauty out of ashes, hope out of despair, love out of loss, and peace out of sorrow. You have eyes even for the broken seeds—the lost, the dormant, the too-far buried—and never give up on a fallow field, no matter how empty. My song is but a meager one, but, nevertheless, I offer it up to you.

From it, I pray you allow something beautiful to grow.

ABOUT THE AUTHOR

Or

The Farmer and His Harvest

CORY KRUSE has worked as an English teacher, fundraiser, marketing communications specialist, and, most recently, as a sales trainer for a local IT company. A graduate of the University of Nebraska, he now resides in South Dakota, where he spends his free time with friends and family, watching college sports, and nerding out over all things *Star Wars*. Along with *Grace in the Dirt*, Kruse is the author of the supernatural suspense novel *A Dream of Darkness*.

Learn more at AuthorCoryKruse.com.

www.ingramcontent.com/pod-product-compliance
Lightning Source LLC
Chambersburg PA
CBHW020511080526
44583CB00013B/565